Amazing
Circular Weaving

Amazing Circular Weaving

LITTLE LOOM TECHNIQUES, PATTERNS AND PROJECTS
FOR COMPLETE BEGINNERS

EMILY NICOLAIDES

Search Press

Contents

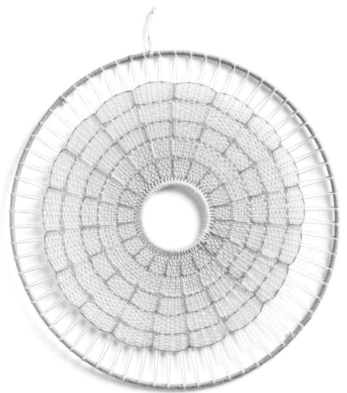

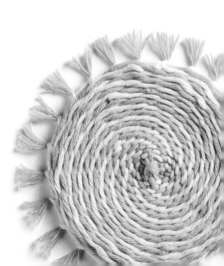

Meet Emily

Hi there!

Thank you for picking up this book. Before we begin weaving, I'd like to introduce myself. My name is Emily Nicolaides. I'm a Cypriot–American artist and weaver. I fell in love with weaving the first moment I sat at a loom in 2013, though my journey with fibre art began long before then.

My invitation into fibre art came from my grandmothers. My maternal grandmother, my Grandmere, was an avid crocheter. She could make anything but particularly loved making blankets, booties and hats for the more than thirty babies she fostered throughout her life. I loved watching her crochet, so when I was old enough, she gave me my first hook and taught me how to do it, too.

My paternal grandmother, my Yiayia Ioulia, loved to knit, needlepoint and make Cypriot-style lace. She doesn't speak much English, and especially as a child my Greek wasn't very good either. Despite the language barrier, she taught me how to knit one winter when she and my grandfather were visiting my family in Virginia. I remember going to the craft store with her and picking out the most putrid shade of green acrylic yarn. She taught me how to make a scarf that winter and despite my terrible colour choice, I loved it so much.

After my grandmothers shared these skills with me, I didn't think much of it. Knitting and crochet were simply activities I enjoyed doing from time to time.

Then one day while sitting in a lecture during my last year of university, it hit me. After four years of art history classes, I had always been drawn to textiles on the rare occasions that textiles were covered. In addition, I was just beginning to see the absurd hierarchies in the art world that impact how different media are valued. This realization was upsetting. I knew deep within me that the skills my grandmothers passed down to me were incredibly meaningful and a part of a global tradition spanning tens of thousands of years. So after a series of ceramic sculptures I made for my senior thesis work exploded, I knew it was time to change medium and explore the art of my matriarchs, fibre art.

A few weeks after graduation, I found myself in a weaving workshop and instantly fell in love with the sounds, feelings and textures of weaving. I loved how the warp and weft crossed and intersected to make cloth, something so much stronger and more impactful than the individual fibres themselves. It felt much like my two grandmothers of different backgrounds, cultures and languages coming together to make me who I am today. Weaving felt like wholeness, family and home.

So that's what I've been doing ever since. Weaving.

In this time, I've learned a lot about this form of artistic expression and when I stumbled into circular weaving in 2016, the shape felt even more right. With all of its symbolism of completeness, the infinite and cycles of life, weaving circles has deepened my connection to fibre art.

After years of study, research, experimentation and love for this style of weaving, I'm honoured to share traditional techniques reimagined for a circular format. I hope you not only make something beautiful for yourself, but also that you find something deep and just for you in the process.

Happy weaving,

Emily

P.S. Although my Grandmere has passed on, I had the pleasure of writing this book from Cyprus in my little studio in the garden of my Yiayia's house. She has seen and approved each project in this book.

About This Book

What is weaving?

What is weaving exactly? Let's start at the very beginning.

There are lots of different kinds of fibre art out there such as knitting, crochet, needlepoint, embroidery, lace, punch needle and tatting. They all have their own differences and unique properties. So what makes weaving different from any of those?

In order for fibre art to be weaving, there must be two parts: the warp and the weft.

Before any actual weaving can begin, the loom must first be 'warped'. Think of it like the skeleton of weaving. First yarn is portioned out and stretched tight across the loom, with gaps in between each warp. It's imperative that the yarn used is strong enough to withstand the high tension. Typically yarns made of cotton, hemp or linen are used for the warp, but any strong yarn can work. This part of the process is referred to as 'warping the loom' (see pages 22–33).

The second part of weaving is known as the 'weft'. This can be any yarn or material that can be woven under and over the warps. Sometimes the weft might be the same yarn as the warp, but there is much more freedom in choosing yarn for the weft.

There are lots of different kinds of weaving and applications for weaving out there. No matter where you go in the world, there is a unique history of weaving for that region. This means that there are many types of looms, fibres, colours, patterns and methods that have evolved over tens of thousands of years! So when you engage in weaving, you're participating in a rich and global tradition of cloth. Pretty cool, right?

What's different about circular weaving?

If you type 'what is weaving?' into a search engine, you'll see a lot of definitions that include information about horizontal, vertical and ninety-degree angles. That's because traditionally, weaving has largely been about creating rectangular-shaped cloth. There are exceptions to this, of course, especially if you're looking at a craft such as basket weaving (which offers a whole style and history of weaving in itself). In general, the warp is typically described as being the vertical yarn stretched up and down and evenly spaced, while the weft is the yarn woven horizontally from left to right. That means that most traditional patterns are only meant for this style of weaving.

But this is a book completely about circular weaving. So we're going to tweak those terms and definitions in favour of something a little different.

In circular weaving, the warps stretch out from a centre point to the outer edge of the hoop (our version of a loom). The weft is woven around the centre point until it reaches the outer edge or a point of your choosing. The gaps between the warps are also different because the distance between them changes as they stretch out from the centre. These slight differences mean that weaving in a circle must be approached differently, as you'll learn throughout this book.

Part of the beauty of circular weaving is that you don't need a lot of expensive or large equipment to get started, unlike more traditional forms of weaving. We'll use various hoops as looms, which are easy to find in most craft shops or online. You might even have some of the tools already if you've done other forms of fibre art.

What you'll learn in this book

In this book, you'll learn how to overcome the aforementioned challenges of circular weaving through step-by-step projects. We'll cover traditional patterns such as tabby, twill, hand-manipulated lace and rib weave, as well as how to finish and display your weavings.

Each project tackles a few different techniques and patterns to demystify circular weaving so that you can learn and use them in your own way. A glossary of key weaving terms can be found on page 136. If a term is *italicized*, you'll find its definition here. There are small yarn cones featured at the beginning of each project to signify difficulty level. Depending on your comfort level with weaving, take these indicators into consideration before beginning each project. Recommended supplies will also be listed at the beginning of each project.

As with anything new, there is a learning curve to circular weaving. Whether you choose to do one or all of these projects, I hope you find satisfaction in the process of weaving. It can be slow moving at times, so if it makes it more enjoyable for you, I recommend turning on some good music, an audiobook or a cosy movie while you weave.

1
Tools & Materials

Supplies for Circular Weaving

You'll need some supplies before you begin weaving circles. In this section we'll provide an overview of what you'll need, but please see the supplies listed at the beginning of each project for specifics as each project is a little different. Most, if not all, of the supplies listed can be found at your local craft or yarn shop, but feel free to get creative with supplies you may already have!

Looms for circular weaving

A loom is a tool used to keep warps stretched, organized and under tension so that the weft can easily be woven through to create cloth. In circular weaving, the looms are hoops.

There are many options for hoops of any size. My favourite circular looms are wooden embroidery and quilting hoops. They work well because the two hoops allow us to sandwich the warps between them so that they don't move around too much during the weaving process. These come in a variety of sizes. The larger sizes are often referred to as quilting hoops as they are traditionally used for hand quilting.

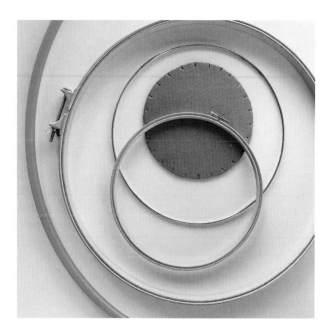

Metal craft hoops, hula hoops, metal bangles, barrel rings or any rigid hoop you might come across can work as a loom, too. In some projects the weaving is left on the hoop for display purposes, so choose hoops carefully in these instances.

How to adjust the featured patterns

Although specific hoop sizes are recommended for most projects in the book, these patterns can be adjusted for larger or smaller sized hoops. If you see a project here that you'd like to make in a different size, I recommend that you first complete the project as shown to get a feel for it.

The easiest projects to adjust are those that specify they can be made with any odd or even number of warps (a note is included under the project dimensions). As a rule of thumb, if you'd like to make a larger version of a project, it will need more warps than indicated. If you'd like to make a smaller version, it will require fewer warps.

Once you're familiar with the patterns, it is also possible to combine them into a single piece. There are endless possibilities for how you can use any of the information in this book for more complex circular weaving, so feel free to get creative!

Individual and doubled-up warps

At the beginning of each project, you'll see 'specifications' listed. This will include the method of warping required for that project, as well as a specific number of warps. While most of the time the total number of warps is flexible if you would like to adjust the size of your hoop, it's important to note whether the project will use individual or doubled-up warps, as this will change how we count our warps.

These terms refer to whether or not you'll need to weave with each individual warp, or if the project requires treating two warps as one (doubled-up). Unless you're using a cardboard loom like in the Swirly Twill Coasters project (page 56), once you warp your hoop there will be two individual warps on top of each other with a gap in between that's created by the edge of the hoop.

There are different occasions to use either individual or doubled-up warps as this affects tension, structure and balance in circular weaving. You'll even learn how to use both within the same piece in projects like the Striped Tabby Cushion (page 42) and the Leno Wall Hanging (page 104).

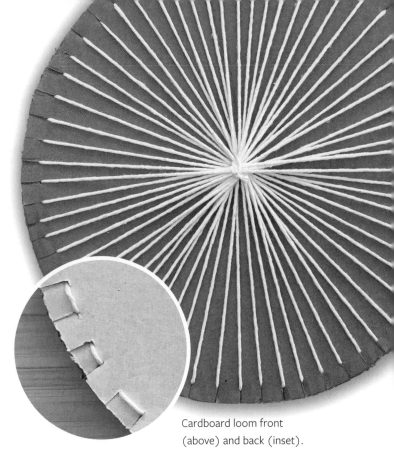

Cardboard loom front
(above) and back (inset).

Cardboard looms

For any projects where the final result is taken off the loom, you can make a cardboard loom. Start by measuring out the correct sized circle and cut it out using a utility knife. With larger projects, such as the Tabby Weave Rag Rug (page 50), the Striped Tabby Cushion (page 42) or the Double Cloth Soumak Cushion (page 62), it's best to cut two circles and hot glue them together. Then cut small equidistant slits around the edge for the correct number of warps.

When it is time to warp your cardboard loom (see pages 22–33), tie one end of the warp in a knot and place it in a slit. Stretch the yarn across to the opposite side, then around the notch to the side and back across.

The Swirly Twill Coasters (page 56) are designed to be made on a cardboard loom – please see the template on page 140 to create your own circle that is 19.5cm (7¾in) in diameter. It has the correct number of slits indicated for the number of warps for this project.

Tapestry needles

Tapestry needles are typically made of metal or plastic and have large, long eyes and blunt tips. I prefer the metal variety because the plastic ones may snap with heavy use or age. There are many varieties and sizes of these needles but there are three main kinds you'll need throughout this book:

A. Extra-long tapestry needle. These needles help speed up the weaving process for larger projects as they allow you to weave longer sections before you need to pull the weft through.

B. Straight tapestry needle. These are the easiest tapestry needles to find and will work well for most projects in this book.

C. Bent tapestry needle. These needles allow you to rock the needle back and forth as you weave over and under warp threads. They are helpful for projects where the warps are very close together. Some people find these needles more comfortable to use than other needles.

The projects in this book will recommend certain needles, but ultimately, you should choose the needle that feels best to you.

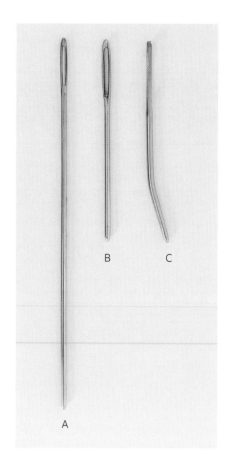

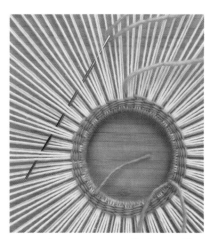

A. Extra-long tapestry needle (as used for Diamond & Fringe Wall Hanging, page 90)

B. Straight tapestry needle (as used for Twisted Warps Wall Hanging, page 112)

C. Bent tapestry needle (as used for Swirly Twill Coasters, page 56)

Stick shuttles

Shuttles are tools used to lead the weft over and under the warps. There are many different kinds of shuttles. In this book we'll use mostly tapestry needles and sometimes stick shuttles.

The Tabby Weave Rag Rug (page 50) recommends using a stick shuttle. These kinds of shuttles are great for larger projects that utilize chunkier materials. In this case, the weft is long strips of fabric. The stick shuttle will allow you to wind the weft material between the notches. These kinds of shuttles are typically made of wood, but please see the template on page 141 for creating a cardboard version.

I recommend cutting out two templates and hot gluing the pieces of sturdy cardboard together to make the shuttle last longer.

Yarns

Throughout this book, weights and fibres of yarn are recommended for each project. Although traditional weaving yarn has its own system of measuring thickness, the yarns in this book will use knitting weights. This is because knitting yarn is easier to find and most craft stores use this system of measurement. Here are the yarn weights you will find in this book:

A. Super fine
B. Light
C. Medium
D. Chunky
E. Super chunky

The warp yarns recommended for this book will all be cotton. This is because cotton yarn is often strong enough to withstand the tension required for a balanced warp.

You will have more freedom choosing weft yarns and can use anything from cotton to wool to acrylic to fabric scraps, although some projects like the Swirly Twill

Coasters (page 56) are better suited to using the same yarn for warp and weft. The specific yarns I used for each project are listed on page 137, if you would like to recreate the projects exactly as they appear.

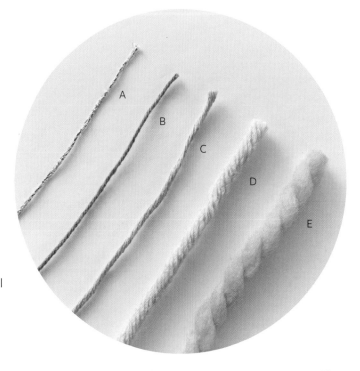

Rings

Fused-metal rings are used for all the open-centre projects, as well as the Twill Woven Bunting (page 36). These rings are a smaller version of the metal craft rings mentioned in Supplies for Circular Weaving (see page 14). Metal bangles and bracelets can also work well as centre rings if these are easier for you to find.

Regardless of the type of rings you choose for these projects, it is important that the rings are fused together. If there is a gap in the ring, when put under tension it will likely open up, creating a frustrating gap for your warps to fall through.

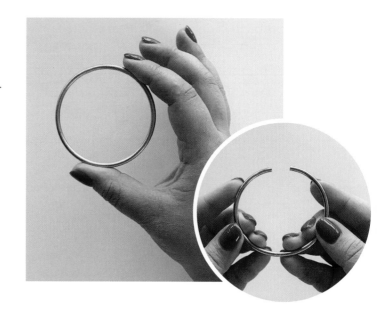

Scissors

Scissors are another important tool you'll need for all the projects in this book. I recommend that you have a pair of sharp scissors set aside just for cutting yarn. When you cut paper or anything else, it will dull the blades. For example, when cutting the fringe in projects like the Diamond & Fringe Wall Hanging (page 90), it will be much easier to cut clean lines if you have very sharp scissors. If possible, I recommend investing in a good pair of scissors as they'll last you a lifetime.

Other Supplies

Other supplies you'll need for this book are clear tape, clothes pegs, a sewing needle, sewing thread, cloth, fabric, pins, fibre cushion stuffing, yarn scraps, spray paint, a pencil or chalk and a ruler. You may already have these lying around your home, but if not you'll need to gather them before starting projects that require these tools.

Circular Weaving Charts

Every project in this book is broken down into manageable steps, each with an accompanying photograph to show you how it's done. For some projects, you'll also find circular weaving charts to help give a different visual representation of the patterns. The charts show the radial warps (in black), and the over and under pattern of the weft (in colour).

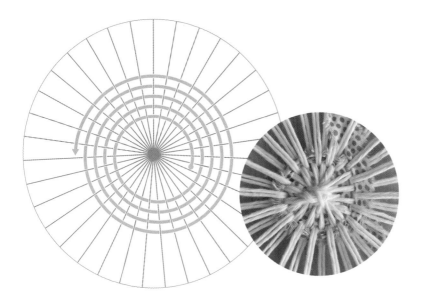

For example...

The Tabby Weave Rag Rug (page 50) uses a simple tabby pattern where the weft is woven over one warp, under one warp. The chart (left) illustrates how this pattern continues as you weave out from the centre.

You'll notice a dot close to the centre. This indicates where the weft yarn begins. In your weaving, this is where the tail end of yarn will be on the backside.

Then you have five passes of tabby that ends with an arrow. This indicates that the weft keeps going.

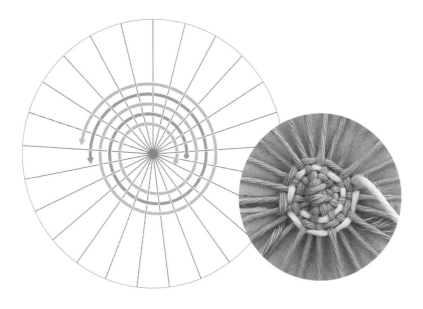

Another example...

The Swirly Twill Coasters (page 56) use two different wefts at the same time. These are indicated in the chart (left) with two different colours: yellow and grey.

Both weft yarns use the same twill pattern, over two warps, under one. However, they are staggered to create the swirl pattern. Please note the dots close to the centre that indicate how the passes should be staggered to achieve the swirly pattern. Again, this is where the weft will begin on the frontside. On your project, your ends will be to the back between these warps.

2

How to Warp any Hoop

An Introduction to Warping

Before we begin weaving over and under, round and round, there must first be something to weave through. Something that creates structure, like a skeleton. In weaving, this structure is achieved through the warp. This term refers to the yarn that is stretched across the hoop or loom before the weaving process begins. In this chapter, you will learn how to turn any hoop into a circular loom for weaving through a process called 'warping the loom'.

There are two main ways to warp a hoop for circular weaving. The first is to warp a hoop where all the warps cross in the middle. This is referred to as a closed-centre warp (see page 26). The second is to warp a hoop in a way where all the warps line up next to each other, around a centre ring. This is my signature technique and a method I spent five years researching and developing before writing this book. I refer to this technique as an open-centre warp (see page 30). Because of the neatness that a centre ring provides, we can weave more complicated and advanced patterns that otherwise wouldn't be possible with the more common closed-centre warp.

There is a third way to warp a hoop that we'll look at in the Twisted Warps Wall Hanging project. This method does not have many applications, so it will be covered in that project on page 112.

Throughout both of the foundational tutorials on closed- and open-centre warps, I have demonstrated on wooden embroidery hoops. Having two rings to sandwich the warps between makes for a more secure circular loom while giving the freedom to have as many or few warps as necessary for a project. A wooden hoop also makes an excellent frame to hang on a wall, as well as being reusable for projects that are meant to be cut off the loom. I have also included tips for warping metal rings and cardboard looms in the tutorials, because some projects in this book work better on different loom types. Feel free to experiment on any sort of circular hoop or ring you may find. I've had great success with hula hoops and circular picture frames as outer hoops, and metal bangles or brackets for inner hoops.

If a project requires a specific kind of loom, it will be noted at the beginning of the tutorial. Consider these warp tutorials as a reference for each project. I recommend practising each warping technique before beginning a specific project because there is much to learn by feel. When you're ready to start a new project, read the specifications listed at the beginning to find out whether the design requires an open or closed centre, if it requires a specific number of warps and whether the project will require single or doubled-up warps. Then refer to this chapter for the step-by-step instructions for the relevant warping method.

Lastly, before we begin it is important to consider the type of yarn used for warping. In general, I recommend using one hundred per cent cotton Aran-weight or thinner yarn. If a project requires a different yarn for the warp, it will be mentioned under the supplies list. Whatever yarn you choose, it must pass the strength test (see opposite).

Let's begin.

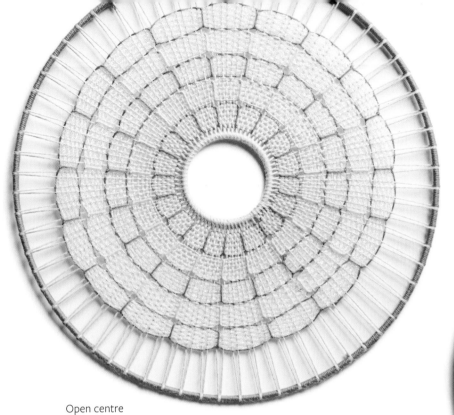

Open centre

Twisted Warps
Wall Hanging

yarn strength test

To test if your yarn is strong enough to withstand the tension of the warp, take one end and wrap it around your index finger twice and then wrap another section around your other index finger. Give it a tug. If it snaps, do not use this yarn for the warp and instead save it to use as weft. If it does not snap, it will be strong enough to withstand the required tension.

Closed centre

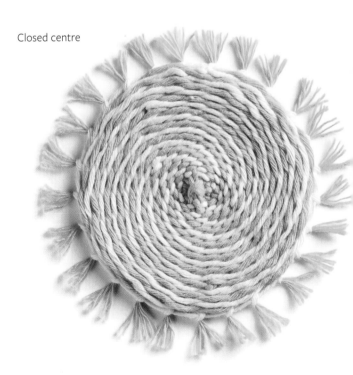

Yarn Butterflies

It can be cumbersome, if not impossible, to handle a whole ball, cone or skein of yarn during the warping process. We can break down our yarn into bundles called *yarn butterflies*, small enough to fit in one hand comfortably and unravel easily. Each project will recommend more yarn butterflies than are necessary because it's always better to have more yarn prepared in case you run out.

SUPPLIES

100 per cent cotton Aran-weight yarn, roughly 9m (10yd)

Scissors

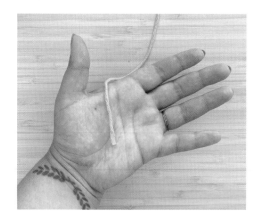

1 Place the cut end of the yarn in the palm of your non-dominant hand with the cut end pointed towards you.

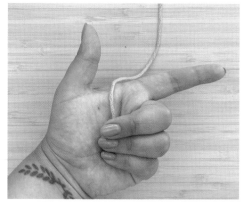

2 Hold the cut end in your palm with your middle, ring and pinky fingers (or whatever feels comfortable to you). Keep your thumb and index finger extended.

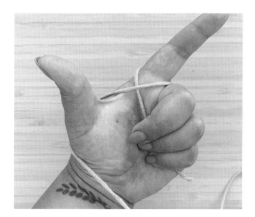

3 Begin wrapping the yarn in a figure-eight pattern. Start by leading the yarn between your thumb and index finger. Then wrap it around your index finger. Next, cross the yarn between your fingers and wrap it around your thumb. You want to see an X-shape between your fingers.

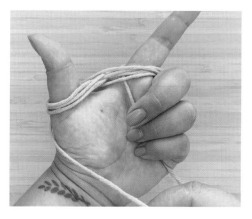

4 Continue wrapping the yarn back and forth around your thumb and index finger in a figure-eight pattern. Once you've wrapped the yarn a couple of times, you can let go of the cut end in the palm of your hand. Keep an eye on this cut end as it will be important later.

5 Continue wrapping. If it starts to feel uncomfortable or tight, you may be pulling the yarn too tightly. Stop wrapping before you completely cover your thumb.

6 Now that you've finished wrapping, close your fingers slightly and pinch the middle where the yarns crossed. Gently slide the bundle of yarn off your hand.

7 Grasping one end of the butterfly with your non-dominant hand, wrap the yarn around the centre three or four times. Be mindful of the cut end that started in the palm of your hand. This will become important shortly.

8 Cut the yarn from the main yarn source. Tuck that end under one of the wraps at the centre.

9 To use the yarn butterfly, pull from the end that started in the palm of your hand. You'll see the yarn gently unravel from the butterfly. Never pull from the end that's wrapped around the centre. If you do, the yarn butterfly will quickly unravel.

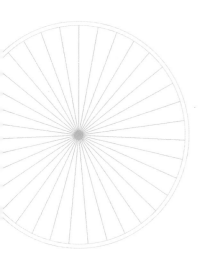

Warping a Hoop With a Closed Centre

About half of the projects in this book are made using the closed-centre warping method. You can use this method on any kind of circular hoop, whether you use an embroidery hoop, metal ring, hula hoop or cardboard loom. I have demonstrated this technique on an embroidery hoop, but please refer to page 15 if you are using a cardboard loom. The following steps will be the same for any project using a closed centre.

SUPPLIES

Embroidery hoop, metal hoop, or cardboard loom

Two yarn butterflies (see page 24)

Clothes peg

Scissors

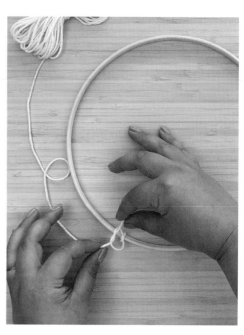

1 Start by removing the outer part of the embroidery hoop from the inner hoop. Set the outer hoop with the screw to the side. If you're using some other kind of ring or a cardboard loom, skip this step.

2 Tie the first yarn butterfly onto the hoop using a simple double knot (see page 138). Pull tight, bringing the knot to the inside of the hoop. If you're using a cardboard or peg loom, tie it onto one of the notches.

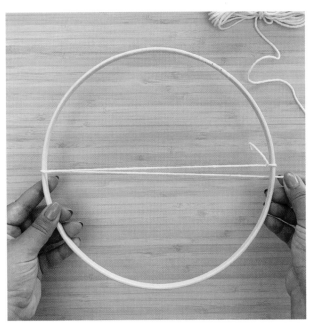

3 Lead the yarn straight across the hoop to the opposite side. Don't pull the yarn so tight that the hoop starts to warp. If warping a metal hoop, wrap the yarn around the hoop edge once before moving onto the next step.

4 Wrap the yarn around to the back. Lead the yarn back to the side of the hoop you tied onto and rotate about 1cm (½in) to the side.

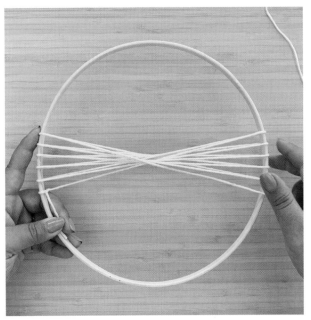

5 Work your way back the other way by leading the yarn across the hoop to the opposite side about 1cm (½in) from the last warp. Don't worry about getting perfect measurements between the warps. A visual estimate is fine. With each new warp you add, place your finger against the yarn and the wooden hoop to hold the tension.

6 Continue wrapping back and forth. Once you've built up a few warps, check the tension by running a finger across the warps. You want them to be flexible but not slide around on the hoop.

7 If you run out of yarn (you will for larger projects or those that require more warps), pin the warp to the edge of the hoop with a clothes peg. Then tie the second yarn butterfly to the existing yarn with an overhand knot (see page 138). Give it a tug before you get back to warping the hoop.

8 Continue wrapping until you reach the place you started. Before you end, pin the warp to the edge of the hoop with the clothes peg again and count the number of warps. Add or subtract whatever you need for the particular project by sliding the warps around as needed.

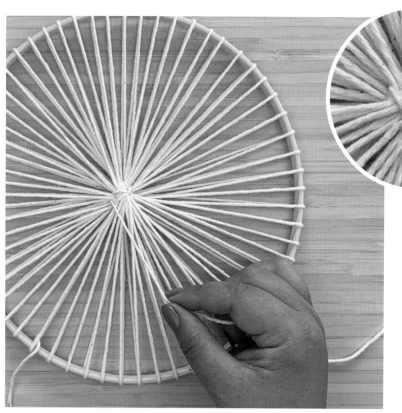

9 Cut the yarn, leaving about 30cm (12in) and wrap one last warp in the same place you tied on. This will give you three separate warps here. Take the remaining yarn and wrap it around the centre where all the warps cross. Using a criss-cross pattern, lead your yarn around the centre, pulling tight to gather the warps into a centre point.

10 Wrap the end around a warp twice to tie a knot. This will be the backside of the weaving. Trim the end as needed.

warp spacing

Don't get hung up on perfectly spacing your warps. Relatively even spacing will get the job done so you can start weaving!

11 Slide the warps around to get the spacing even, if necessary. Then place the outer part of the embroidery hoop back onto the inner hoop. This will hold all the warps in place. Now you're ready to begin weaving.

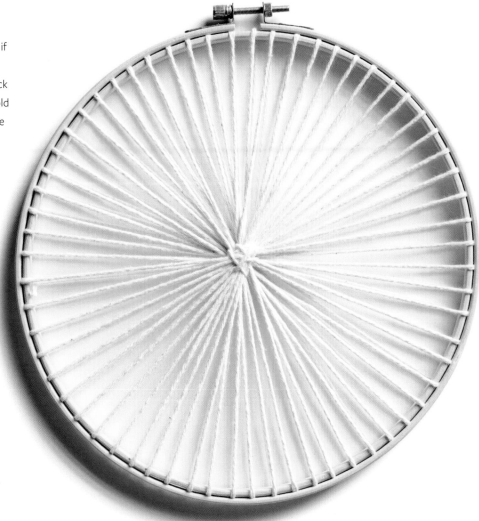

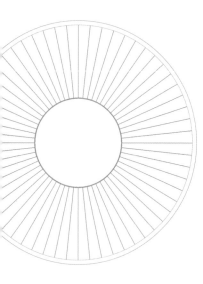

Warping a Hoop With an Open Centre

About half of the projects in this book are made using the open-centre warping method. You can use this method on any type of hoop, although I will demonstrate it on an embroidery hoop. This method is not so conducive to weaving on a cardboard loom as it is too cumbersome to pass a yarn butterfly through the centre ring with the cardboard at the backside. The following steps will be the same for any project using an open centre.

SUPPLIES

Embroidery hoop or metal hoop

100 per cent cotton Aran-weight yarn for the supplementary ties

Two yarn butterflies (see page 24)

Small metal ring

Ruler

Clothes peg

Scissors

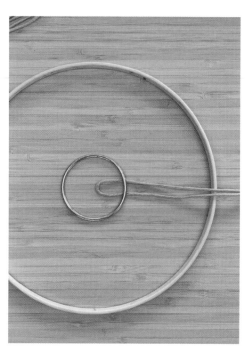

1 Start by removing the outer part of the embroidery hoop from the inner hoop. Set the outer hoop with the screw to the side. If you're using some other kind of ring or a cardboard loom, skip this step. Using yarn in a different colour than the warp, measure out a piece of yarn that's double the width of the hoop and cut. Use this as a guide to cut three more yarn pieces of the same length and set aside.

2 Place the small metal ring at the centre of the hoop. Fold one of the cut pieces of yarn in half. Place the looped end underneath the ring.

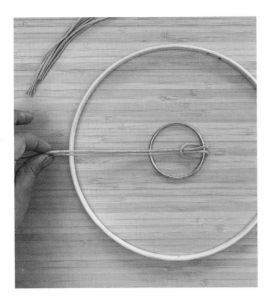

3 Pull the two cut ends through the loop of yarn. Pull tight to create a lark's head knot (see page 139).

4 Repeat this process for the other three pieces of yarn. Move the knots so that they are positioned around the ring as shown. These will be *supplemental ties* to suspend the ring in the centre of the hoop. Think of them like scaffolding as they will be cut off when they are no longer needed.

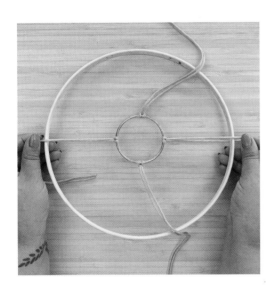

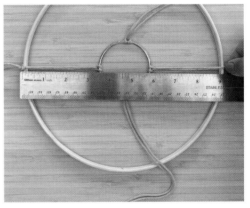

5 On the right side, separate the two ends placing one underneath the hoop, and one on top. Repeat on the left side. Then pinch the two ends together on either side, on the outside of the hoop. Pull these two supplementary ties taut and centre the ring in the middle of the hoop.

6 When the ring appears centred, pinch as close to the edge of the hoop on either side as you can. Let go of one side and tie a loose overhand knot (see page 138). You want the knot to be a little loose in case you need to adjust the placement. Then gently pull the untied supplementary tie to suspend the ring. Using a ruler, measure the distance between the hoop and ring on either side. I aim to get the measurement within 6mm (¼in) of difference. When you get the ring more or less centred, tie a double knot (see page 138) on the other side and tighten the first knot.

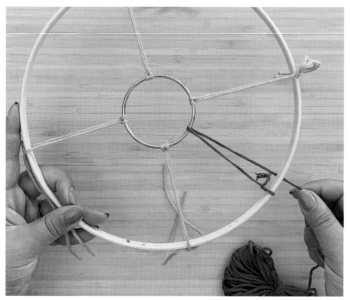

7 Repeat this with the other two ties. These will be much easier than the first two as the ring is already suspended at the centre.

8 Now that the supplementary ties are in place, tie a yarn butterfly onto the outer hoop. Pull the knot tight. Then lead the yarn butterfly towards the centre and through the ring to the back. Once through the ring, lead the yarn back to the outer edge where you started and move about 1cm (½in) from the last warp. I prefer to work anticlockwise but move in whatever direction feels more natural to you.

9 Continue wrapping around the outer hoop and inner hoop. Each time you create a new warp, place the thumb of your non-dominant hand against the yarn and hoop to keep the tension. Be careful that the warps do not cross over each other at the centre. You want the warps to be one next to the other.

10 Continue wrapping. As you approach the first supplementary warp, simply move it to the side. If it feels too tight, you may cut it off altogether.

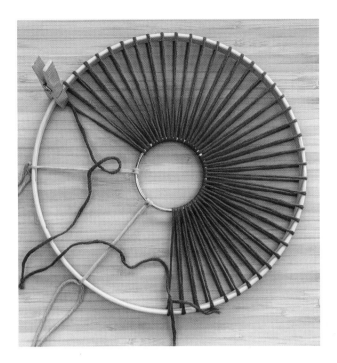

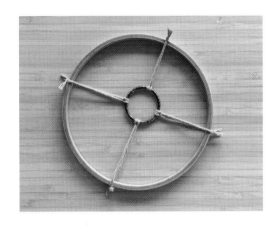

off-centre warp

With open-centre weaving, the ring does not have to be centred. If you'd like to create an off-centre warp, as in the Crescent Moon Wall Hanging (page 130), simply tie your supplemental ties at different lengths before you begin warping.

11 When it's time to tie on a new yarn butterfly, pin the last warp wrapped to the hoop with a clothes peg. Then tie on the next yarn butterfly using an overhand knot (see page 138). Continue wrapping. Cut the supplementary ties when you have enough warps to suspend the ring on its own.

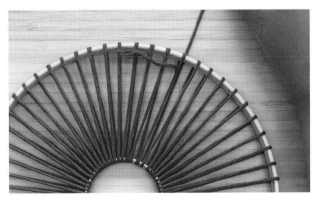

12 When you've wrapped almost all the way around, pin the last warp to the hoop and count the warps. Add or subtract warps as needed, sliding the existing ones around. Then when you have the right amount, tie the last warp at the same place you started using a double knot (see page 138).

13 Work around the hoop, adjusting the warps for even spacing. Then place the outer hoop back onto the inner hoop to hold the warps in place. Now you are ready to begin your project.

3

For the Home

Twill Woven Bunting

This project uses a technique called *twill* to create lovely swirly weavings. You'll also learn how to add fringe using lark's head knots. Then we'll attach them to a long string, making it easy to hang your woven bunting wherever you like. This is a great way to add colour to your home or bring a little something extra to a party!

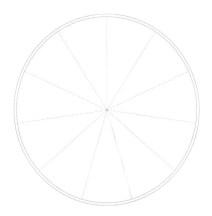

Project dimensions:
Bunting 1.5m (1½yd) in length;
each weaving 6cm (2½in)
in diameter

Note: *This twill pattern can be adjusted for any size hoop. Your total number of doubled-up warps must be a multiple of 3, minus 1. For example 14, 26 or 59 doubled-up warps would work for this project.*

SPECIFICATIONS

Closed-centre method
(see page 26)

11 doubled-up warps

SUPPLIES

Spray paint for metal (optional)

10 x 6-cm (2½-in)
fused-metal rings

Scissors

Ruler

Tapestry needle

100 per cent cotton medium-weight yarn for the warp, roughly 13.5m (15yd)

Any yarn in the weight and fibre of your choice for the weft (I chose three colours of medium-weight wool), roughly 45m (50yd) in total

1 If the colour of your rings does not match the colour palette you'd like, it's very easy to paint them with spray paint meant for metal. Be sure to do this outside and use light coats. Allow the paint to dry between coats. If you like the colour of your rings, skip this step.

2 Warp the first ring using the closed-centre method (see page 26) and 11 doubled-up warps. There is no need to make yarn butterflies for a hoop this small. For a 6-cm (2½-in) fused-metal ring, you need about 1.5m (1½ yd) of warp yarn.

3 Measure out about 3.5m (4yd) of yarn. If you chose weft that's chunky or super chunky weight, measure out one length of yarn. If you're using anything thinner, I suggest measuring out at least two. I used two lengths of Aran-weight yarn in different colours. Now double up however many strands you cut. Loop the yarn around one of the warps at the halfway point. Thread the cut ends through the eye of the tapestry needle.

4 Now let's begin weaving a twill pattern. Use the needle to begin weaving **over two warps, under one warp**. Then repeat **over two, under one**. Use the end of the needle to pack the weft down closer to the centre knot.

5 Continue weaving. As you work your way out from the centre, you'll notice the swirl begin to emerge. Keep weaving until you reach the outer edge.

6 When you're done weaving, it's time to hide the tail of the yarn. Take the threaded needle and run it along the last warp you wove, underneath the weft. Pull the needle and yarn through. Trim any ends.

7 Let's prepare the trim. Measure out 12 pieces of yarn at 20cm (8in) each. Cut to size and arrange in three groups of four.

8 Now let's attach the fringe to the hoop using a lark's head knot (see page 139). Fold the first group of yarn in half. Thread the looped end from the front of the weaving to the back, between two warps. The loop should be facing away from the weaving.

9 Then take all the cut ends and thread them through the loop. Pull the ends away from the weaving to tighten. Repeat steps 8–9 to make two more fringes.

10 Now trim the fringes to the preferred length. Make sure to use your sharpest scissors to get a clean cut.

fringe length

When you begin trimming the fringe, leave it longer than you think you'd like. You can always cut it shorter, but you can't make it longer!

11 Now that you have completed one and have a feel for the process, I suggest batch making the rest of the mini weavings by warping the other nine hoops, then weaving nine, then preparing all the fringe, then adding the fringe. Batching will make your individual weavings more consistent and speed up the process.

12 The last step is to attach the mini weavings to the hanging string to create your bunting. Measure out a piece of yarn (I used the same colour as my warp) to about 1.5 m (1½ yd). Tie each mini weaving to the string using a cow hitch (see page 139). Do your best to space the weavings 10cm (4in) apart. It's easier to get the spacing right if you tie the knot first and then loosen it to adjust the spacing.

'Now you're ready to hang your woven bunting! If you enjoyed this project, you can always make more mini weavings for longer bunting. If you liked weaving twill, I highly recommend checking out the Swirly Twill Coasters on page 56 for a slightly more advanced project.'

Striped Tabby Cushion

In this project, you'll weave a subtle rippling pattern to create a circular cushion for your favourite chair. If you save your weaving scraps like I do, this is a great project to put them to use. Plus, you'll learn how to navigate the challenges of weaving on a larger scale. Basic sewing skills are useful for this project.

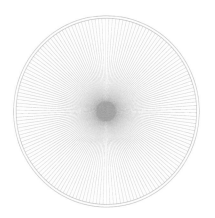

Project dimensions:
35cm (14in) in diameter

Note: *It is not recommended to adjust the total number of individual warps for this project due to the pattern used.*

SPECIFICATIONS

Closed-centre method
(see page 26)

162 individual warps

SUPPLIES

46-cm (18-in) wooden embroidery hoop (sometimes hoops of this size are referred to as quilting hoops)

Extra-long tapestry needle (if you can't find this then any tapestry needle will work fine)

Ruler

Scissors

50 x 50-cm (20 x 20-in) piece of fabric (I suggest a neutral colour like black or white)

Pen, pencil or chalk to mark the fabric

Pins

Sewing needle

Sewing thread in the same colour as the fabric

Fibre cushion stuffing and/or yarn scraps, about 0.5kg (1lb) in weight

100 per cent cotton medium-weight yarn for the warp, roughly 90m (100yd)

Medium-weight wool yarn (or the fibre of your choice) in four colours for the weft, roughly 90m (100yd) of each

1 Warp the hoop using the closed-centre method (see page 26) and 162 individual warps.

2 Thread the extra-long tapestry needle with about 1m (1yd) of the weft colour of your choice. Using a criss-cross pattern, weave back and forth over the centre knot.

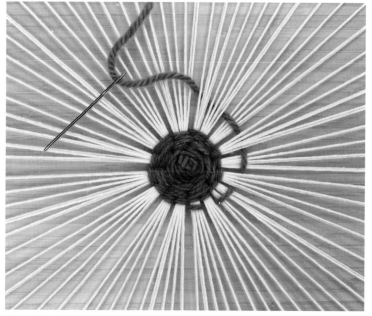

3 Once covered, weave choppy, long stitches around the centre knot until the width of the centre is at least 5cm (2in). It doesn't matter how many warps you weave over and under as long as the weft mostly covers the warp.

4 Switch yarns to the colour of your choice. Thread the tapestry needle with about 1m (1yd) of yarn. Picking up where you left off, begin weaving *tabby* **over three warps, under three warps**. Weave between three and twenty passes to create your first stripe. You'll notice the pattern reverses with each pass because of the odd number of warps. The reason why we are grouping the warps in this way is that the warps are so close together. We'll change this later when we have more space in between them.

flip it over

yarn tails

Whenever the yarn is running low or you need to switch colours, leave yourself a tail on the backside that's at least 2.5cm (1in) in length. Then rethread the needle and pull the yarn from the back to the front where you left off.

5 Now let's weave a wavy line. Switch to a contrasting colour and weave two passes using the same **over three, under three** pattern. As you add these wavy lines throughout the weaving, you'll notice a lovely ripple pattern begins to form.

6 Switch colours and weave between three and twenty passes to create a stripe. Continue alternating stripes and wavy lines in your preferred thicknesses until the width of the woven circle is about 20cm (8in). Experiment with thick and thin stripes and notice how wide the beads become, the further you move out from the centre.

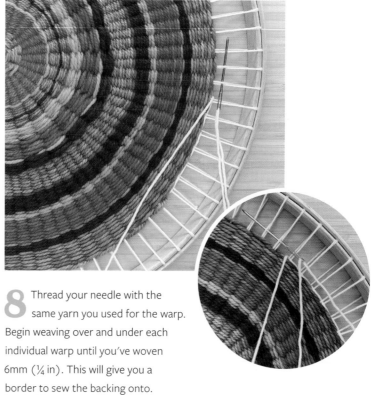

7 As the warps are now farther apart, let's adjust our tabby pattern. Doubling up on the warps, switch colours and begin weaving tabby **over one warp, under one warp**. You'll notice that the weave feels tighter, so be careful not to pull or pack the weft too tightly. Continue until the weaving is 35cm (14in) wide.

8 Thread your needle with the same yarn you used for the warp. Begin weaving over and under each individual warp until you've woven 6mm (¼ in). This will give you a border to sew the backing onto.

9 Remove the outer hoop and trim the warps around the edge. You'll need to do this on a table as the ends have not yet been secured.

10 To finish the warp ends, tie two together in a double knot (see page 138) all around the edge of the weaving.

flip it over

11 Flip the weaving over so that the backside is facing up. Tie any loose weft ends together in a double knot and trim.

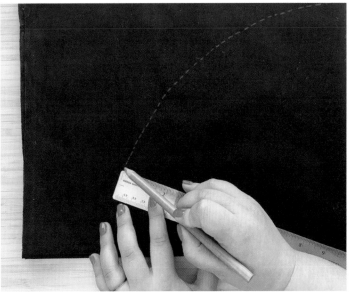

12 Take the fabric you'll use for the back of the cushion and fold it in half, then in half again. Measure 25cm (10in) from the folded point and mark a quarter circle. Cut all four pieces of fabric along the marks.

13 Unfold the fabric and place the circle flat on the table. Then place the weaving in the centre of the circle, backside up. Fold the white edge of the weaving inwards. Then fold the fabric over that edge. Pin through the white border and to the front of the fabric.

14 Thread the sewing needle with the sewing thread and stitch the fabric to the edge of the woven border. Stitch through all the layers, folding the fabric in as you go. Leave an opening of about 13cm (5in). Turn right side out.

15 Stuff the cushion with fibre cushion stuffing and/or yarn scraps, including the ones from this project. A mix of both gives the cushion a nice weight. To test, set the cushion on its side. If it looks droopy, keep stuffing. Then hand stitch the opening closed and pat to distribute evenly.

'Now you're ready to enjoy this cushion on your sofa or favourite chair! If you'd like to make a slightly more advanced cushion next, check out the project on page 62.'

Tabby Weave Rag Rug

In this project, you'll learn how to weave a rug with fabric scraps using a classic weaving pattern called *tabby*. Because the pattern is simply over one, under one, it can be really soothing and meditative to weave. Plus, the chunky material makes it a quick project to weave up once the fabric is prepped.

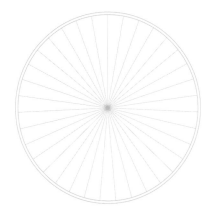

Project dimensions:
59cm (23in) in diameter

Note: *This can be woven on any size of hoop, as long as it is larger than the rug you would like to create – I used a 76-cm (30-in) hula hoop. If you would like to weave a larger or smaller version of this pattern, the total number of doubled-up warps must be odd.*

SPECIFICATIONS

Closed-centre method (see page 26)

35 doubled-up warps

SUPPLIES

76-cm (30-in) hula hoop

Ruler

Scissors

Cardboard shuttle (see template on page 141)

Three to four yarn butterflies made of 100 per cent cotton medium-weight yarn for the warp, roughly 27–36m (30–40yd)

2m (2½ yd) non-stretch cotton fabric for the weft

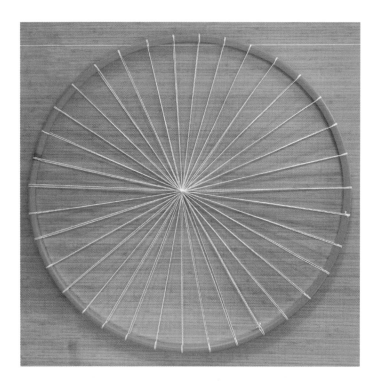

1 Warp the hoop using the closed-centre method (see page 26) and 35 doubled-up warps. I used a hula hoop that is 76cm (30in) across and placed warps about 4cm (1½in) away from each other. If you are using a metal or plastic hoop, the warp will stay in place better if you wrap the yarn around the outside edge twice.

2 Let's prepare our weft. Fold the fabric in half and cut into 2cm (¾in) strips. The strips should be as long as possible. Make sure the fabric is not at all stretchy. If using one hundred per cent cotton, you may be able to cut a small piece, and then tear the fabric into strips.

3 Once you have a pile of fabric strips ready to go, tie the ends together so that you have one long continuous strip of fabric and wrap around the shuttle. You can use the same colour throughout or alternate colours as I did.

old for new

For this project you can use new fabric or repurpose something old. This is a great way to reuse old sheets and pillowcases. Just make sure that the fabric is not stretchy as this will ruin your tension and create problems when you cut the weaving off the hoop.

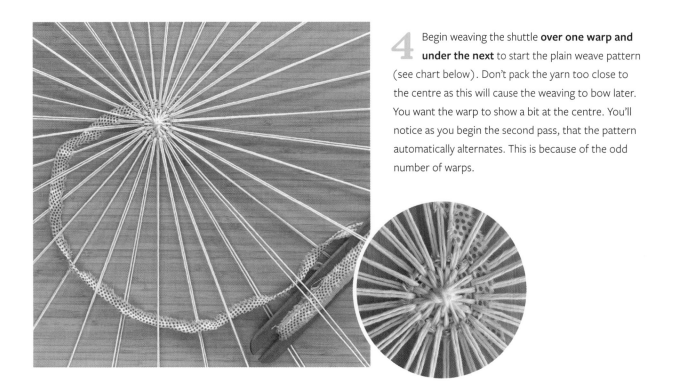

4 Begin weaving the shuttle **over one warp and under the next** to start the plain weave pattern (see chart below). Don't pack the yarn too close to the centre as this will cause the weaving to bow later. You want the warp to show a bit at the centre. You'll notice as you begin the second pass, that the pattern automatically alternates. This is because of the odd number of warps.

tabby weave: over 1, under 1

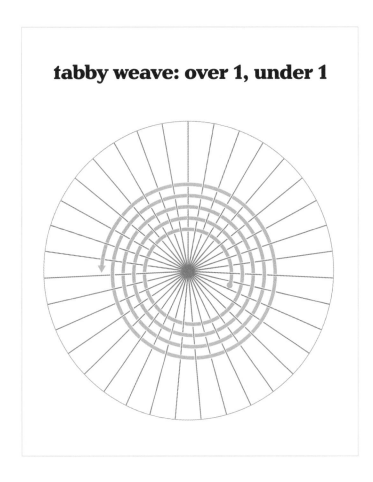

5 As you approach the first knot, do your best to tuck the knotted end between two warps and to the backside of the weaving.

6 Check the tension as you weave – remember to keep the weaving on the looser side. It's okay if the warp continues to show in places.

7 When you've reached the desired width – my rug is 59cm (23in) in diameter – tie the weft onto a warp with a double knot (see page 138) to secure.

8 Next use the same yarn you used for the warp to tie double half hitch knots (see page 138) all the way around the weaving.

9 Now it's time to cut the weaving off the loom. Slide your scissors underneath each warp and snip. Make sure you're doing this step on a flat surface.

10 Separate each doubled-up set of warps. Using a double knot (see page 138), tie one end from each warp to an end from the next set of warps. Work your way all the way around the weaving. Trim the tails. In combination with the half hitch knots, this will prevent the weaving from unravelling.

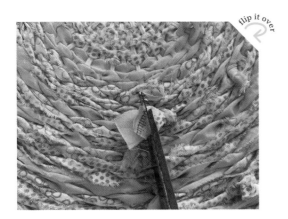

flip it over

11 Turn the rug over and cut any long fabric tails from the weft.

'Flip back over to the front side and you're all done. Great job weaving your circular rug! It will look great next to a bed, in the kitchen or wherever you'd like to add a pop of colour.'

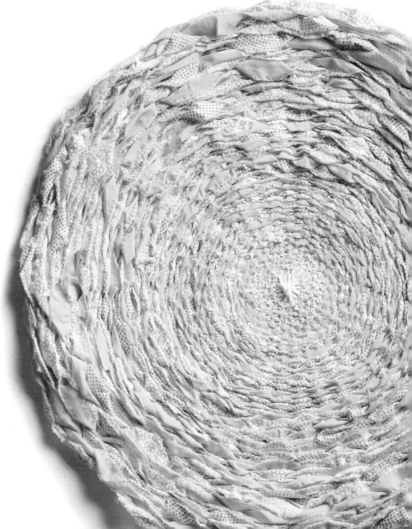

Swirly Twill Coasters

In this project, we'll revisit a classic weaving pattern called *twill*. There are many variations of this pattern but for this project we'll focus on a simple variation called a 2/1 twill pattern. We'll use two contrasting yarn colours to create a swirl that starts from the centre and works its way out. If you enjoy this pattern, I recommend checking out a more advanced twill pattern on page 130.

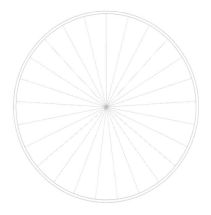

Project dimensions:
9cm (3½in) in diameter

Note: *If you would like to weave a larger or smaller version of this pattern, the total number of warps must be a multiple of 3 plus 1. For example, 13, 19, 25 or 46 individual warps would all work for this project.*

SPECIFICATIONS

Closed-centre method
(see page 26)

25 individual warps on a
cardboard loom

SUPPLIES

19.5-cm (17¾-in) cardboard
loom with 25 notches (see
template on page 140)

Two bent tapestry needles

Scissors

Ruler

Pencil

100 per cent cotton medium-
weight yarn in two contrasting
colours, roughly two 85-m
(93-yd) balls. Use the same kind
of yarn for both warp and weft
for best results.

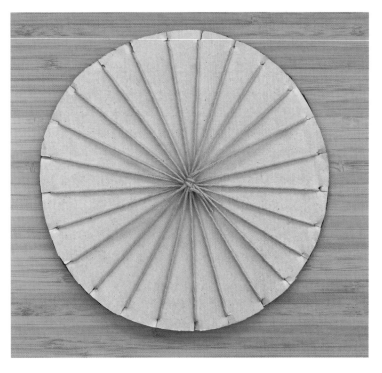

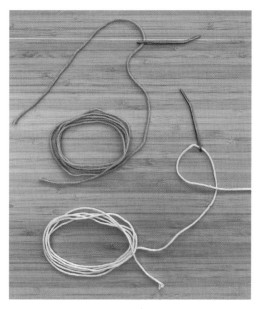

2 Thread two bent tapestry needles with about 1m (1yd) of each yarn colour.

1 Use the template on page 140 to create a cardboard loom with 25 individual warps. An embroidery or metal hoop is not recommended for this project as the double warps will affect the final product. Choose either of the two colours for the warp and warp the hoop using the closed-centre method (see page 26). Yarn butterflies are not necessary for a small loom.

3 Start with the needle threaded with yarn the same colour as the warp. Weave **over two warps, under one** (see chart opposite). Stop weaving before you start the second pass. Leave a tail of about 2.5cm (1in). Tug both ends of the yarn to gently pull the weft to the centre. Then position the tail to the back of the weaving, between the warps and the cardboard.

weft tension

It's important to keep the weft loose while weaving to ensure the coasters are nice and flat. If the weft is packed down too tight, the coasters may turn up at the edges when removed from the loom.

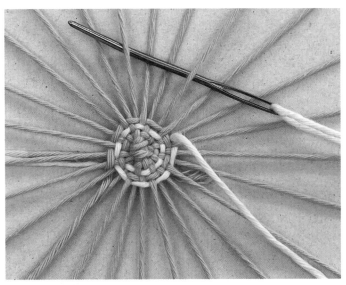

5 Continue weaving this pattern by alternating the colours. The more passes you weave, the more the swirl pattern will begin to emerge.

4 Take the needle threaded with the second colour and repeat same pattern, but start weaving one warp to the left of the start of the first pass. Weave **over two warps, under one.** See the chart (right) for clarification on where each warp begins as this is important to the pattern. Stop weaving before you start the third pass.

6 At some point, you will need to tie on more yarn. Using an overhand knot (see page 138), tie a new cut piece of yarn in the same colour to the end of the first piece of yarn. Tuck the knot to the backside as you continue weaving.

twill weave: over 2, under 1

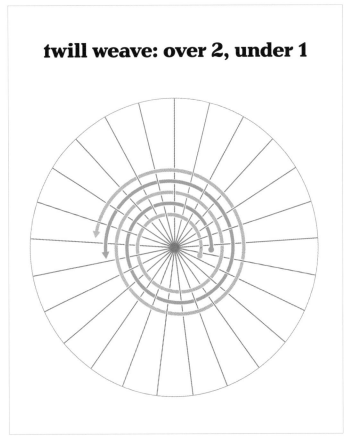

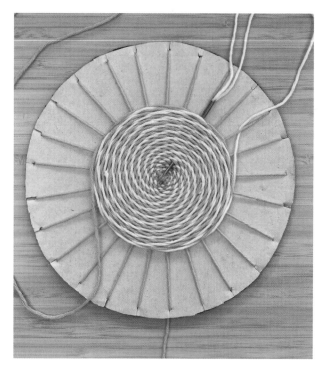

7 When you've woven a circle about 9cm (3½in) in diameter, stop weaving. Tuck one of the colours of yarn into the weaving by running the needle along the closest warp, underneath the weft. Pull the needle all the way through and trim the yarn so that it hides the end in the weaving.

8 Using the other colour of yarn, wrap your needle over and around the next warp. The needle should point in the opposite direction to which you were previously weaving. This is the beginning of a double half hitch knot (see page 138), a tiny knot that will prevent the weaving from unravelling.

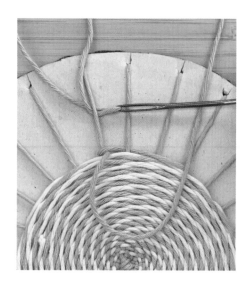

9 Repeat the same wrapping motion on the same warp to create the knot. Pull tight. Repeat this knot on each warp, working in the same direction that you were weaving before.

10 Once you've finished the last half hitch knot, tuck the end into the weaving at the warp where you tied the first knot. Trim the remaining yarn to hide the end in the weaving.

11 In pencil or chalk, mark each warp 2cm (¾in) from the half hitch. This will be the coaster fringe. If you would prefer a longer or shorter fringe, feel free to mark whatever measurement you like.

12 Now it's time to cut the weaving from the loom. Using your sharpest scissors, cut the warps where you marked.

13 Use the end of a tapestry needle to gently comb out the yarn and create the fringe.

'I hope you enjoyed learning twill and double half hitch knots to create these swirly coasters. They make a great gift and you can have fun experimenting with different colour combinations.'

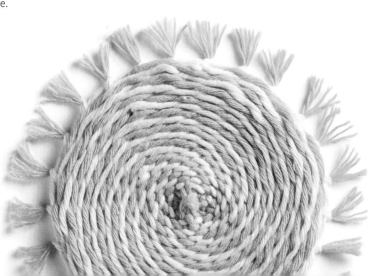

Double Cloth Soumak Cushion

If you enjoyed making the Striped Tabby Cushion on page 42, you'll love this one too! In this project, we'll weave both the front and back of the cushion using a technique called *double cloth*. Basically, we'll create two weavings on the same hoop, using the front warps for one side of the cushion, and the back warps for the other side. You'll also learn a fun braid-like technique called *soumak*. Just to prepare you: this project will take twice as long as the last cushion since we're making two weavings in one!

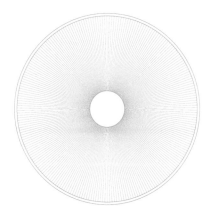

Project dimensions:
35cm (14in) in diameter

Note: *It is not recommended to adjust the total number of individual warps for this project due to the pattern used.*

SPECIFICATIONS

Open-centre method
(see page 30)

234 individual warps

SUPPLIES

46-cm (18-in) wooden embroidery hoop (sometimes hoops of this size are referred to as quilting hoops)

6-cm (2½-in) fused metal ring

Extra-long tapestry needle (if you can't find this then any tapestry needle will work fine)

Ruler

Scissors

Fibre cushion stuffing and/or yarn scraps, about 0.5kg (1lb) in weight

100 per cent cotton medium-weight yarn for the warp, roughly 120m (130yd)

Medium-weight wool yarn in five colours for weft, roughly 180m (200yd) each

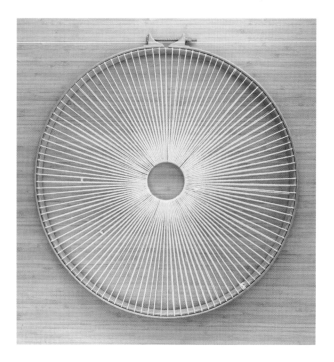

1 Warp the hoop using the open-centre method (see page 30) and 234 individual warps.

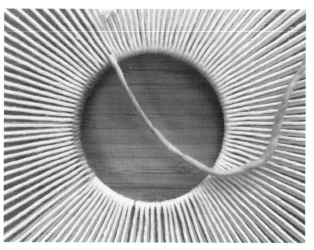

2 Cut about 1m (1yd) of weft yarn in the colour of your choice. Wrap the yarn around the centre ring between the warps. When you've finished wrapping, tie the two ends together in a double knot and leave the tails long. We'll hide these in the weaving later.

3 Now it's time to begin weaving. Measure 1m (1yd) of yarn in the colour of your choice and thread the extra-long tapestry needle. Begin weaving *tabby* on the top warps only. Work **over three, under three**. This will be one side of the cushion. Stop when you've woven about 2.5cm (1in). If you need to add on more yarn, leave the weft ends to the front.

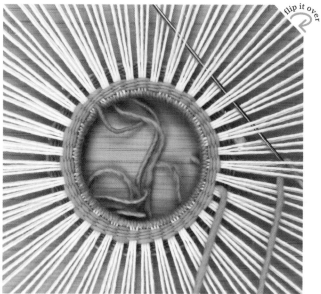

flip it over

4 Flip the weaving over. Measure 1m (1yd) of yarn in the colour of your choice and thread the extra-long tapestry needle. Begin weaving tabby on the back warps only. Again, work **over three, under three**. This will be the other side of the cushion. Flipping your cushion and repeating the pattern in this way will help to keep the warp tension evenly distributed while you work.

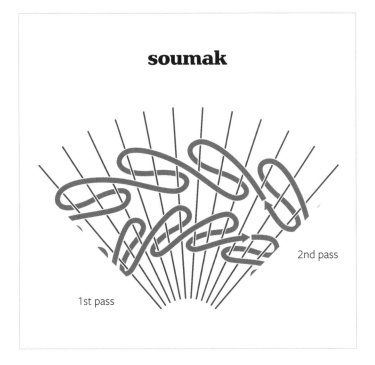

soumak

2nd pass

1st pass

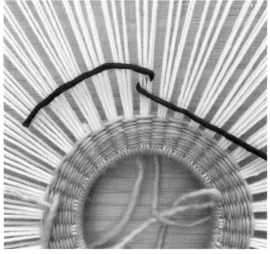

5 Now let's weave some soumak! As with our previous passes of tabby, we will be working with warps in groups of three. Measure 1.75m (2yd) of yarn in the colour of your choice. Wrap the yarn behind one grouping of warps with the short end on top and the long end closer to the centre. A needle is not necessary, but you're welcome to use one if it feels more comfortable.

6 Take the long end and lead it over top of the three warps to the right. Thread the yarn behind the warps and to the left. Pull the yarn to the front before the first wrapped warps. You want the end to poke out between the wrap and the passes of tabby you wove previously. Pull down. The chart above gives a visual guide to weaving soumak.

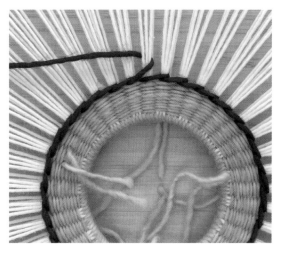

7 Continue this pattern of wrapping the warps. This will be half of the first pass of soumak. When you reach the first warps that you wrapped, simply make a sideways V-shape, as shown.

8 Now we'll work back the other way to create the other half of the first pass of soumak. Repeat the same wrapping motion, but the opposite way. Thread the yarn around and behind the warps to the right. Pull the yarn to the front.

adding yarn

When it's time to add on more yarn, thread the cut ends to the back as shown in step 8.

9 When you reach the end of the soumak, tuck the end to the back. Because you are weaving on the front and back of the weaving, there is a little pocket in between to tuck the ends into. Repeat the soumak on the other side.

flip it over

10 Continue alternating weaving tabby stripes in whatever thickness you like and then a round of soumak. Do this on both sides.

11 When you have woven about 4cm (1½in) from the centre you'll notice more distance between the warps. Begin doubling up the yarn for the soumak.

12 When your weaving measures about 7.5cm (3in), begin weaving tabby **over and under one warp,** instead of groups of three. Also wrap the soumak around one warp instead of three.

14 Stop weaving when your weaving measures about 35cm (14 in). Tie a row of double half hitch knots (see page 138) around one side of the piece, and then the other.

13 When your weaving measures about 10cm (4in), quadruple the yarn for each pass of soumak. This will create a chunkier and more visible soumak.

16 Take one warp from each side of the cushion and tie in a double knot to close. Leave an opening of about 15cm (6in). It needs to be large enough to get your hand into so that you can easily distribute the stuffing.

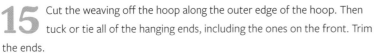

15 Cut the weaving off the hoop along the outer edge of the hoop. Then tuck or tie all of the hanging ends, including the ones on the front. Trim the ends.

17 Stuff the cushion with fibre cushion stuffing and/or yarn scraps. Use small handfuls and make sure to distribute the stuffing evenly around the cushion. Once the cushion is full, tie the remaining warps together in double knots to close the opening.

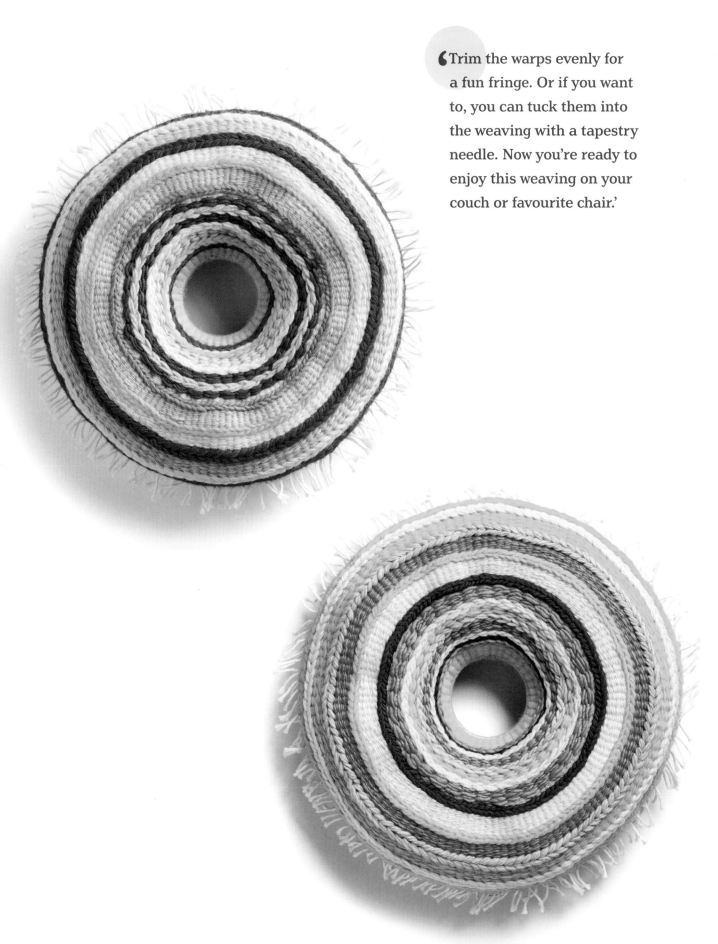

'Trim the warps evenly for a fun fringe. Or if you want to, you can tuck them into the weaving with a tapestry needle. Now you're ready to enjoy this weaving on your couch or favourite chair.'

Circular Placemats

In this project you'll use yarn and metal hoops to create one-of-a-kind placemats for your home. We'll alternate stripes of colour with small radiating sections to create negative space in the weaving. These placemats are a great way to add pops of colour to your daily life or your next dinner party.

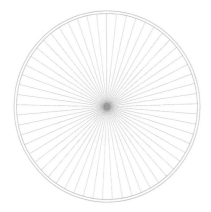

Project dimensions:
30cm (12in) in diameter

Note: *This pattern can be adjusted for any sized hoop. Your total number of doubled-up warps must be a multiple of 3. For example 39, 63 or 87 doubled-up warps would work well for this project.*

SPECIFICATIONS

Closed-centre method
(see page 26)

57 doubled-up warps

SUPPLIES

30-cm (12-inch) metal hoop
(one for each placemat)

Ruler

Scissors

Extra-long tapestry needle (if you can't find this then any tapestry needle will work fine)

Bent tapestry needle

100 per cent cotton medium-weight yarn for the warp, roughly 90m (100yd) per placemat

Medium-weight wool yarn (or the fibre of your choice) in three colours for the weft, roughly 90m (100yd) of each per placemat (you could also use doubled-up thinner weight yarn)

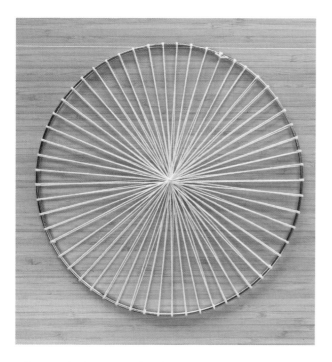

1 Warp the hoop using the closed-centre method (see page 26) and 57 doubled-up warps.

2 Measure out about 5.5m (6yd) of yarn in the first colour of your choice (I chose blush). Wrap it around the outer hoop as per the instructions on page 89.

yarn ends

As you add on more yarn, leave the ends to the back. We'll tuck all the ends into the weaving at the end.

3 Thread the extra-long tapestry needle with the second colour (burnt orange) and begin weaving *tabby* **over three warps, under three warps**. Do your best to pack the weft close to the centre. You will see the warp exposed at the centre for a different look and less bulk.

4 Continue until your weaving measures about 4cm (1½in) from the centre.

5 Thread the bent tapestry needle with about 1m (1yd) in the third colour (white). Begin weaving **under one**, **over one**, **under one**. Then back **over one**, **under one**, **over one** across the same three warps. If you choose something thinner than Aran weight, please double the yarn, as shown.

6 Repeat until you've woven a section 4-cm (1½-in) long (about twenty passes). Then use the needle to tuck the end under the centre weft. Leave the starting ends to the back and we'll tuck these at the end.

7 Repeat steps 5 and 6 until you've completed nineteen rectangles.

9 Switch back to the third colour. Thread the bent tapestry needle with about 1m (1yd) of yarn. Weave **over and under three warps** that correspond to the three-warp sections that you wove in the second row. Again weave sections measuring about 4cm (1½in); about twenty-five passes this time (to compensate for the wider distance between the warps).

8 Now thread the extra-long tapestry needle with about 1m (1yd) of the first colour of yarn. Weave a section of *tabby* (**over one warp, under one warp**) measuring about 4cm (1½in).

10 Repeat eighteen times to complete the row of individually woven rectangles.

11 Thread the extra-long tapestry needle with the second colour of yarn. Weave tabby until you've woven right up to the edge of the metal hoop.

12 Flip the placemat to the backside. Use the bent tapestry needle to tuck all the ends into the weaving. The reason why it's better to tuck them instead of tie the ends together is that when you use the placemat it will lie flat on the table with no bumps for a smooth surface.

'Now repeat for as many placemats as you'd like. Feel free to change the colours around for a unique look!'

4

For the Walls

Sunny Rib Weave Wall Hanging

This sunny wall hanging is created using a variation of tabby weave called *rib weave*. This pattern is traditionally used to create vertical stripes or columns in the cloth. When woven in a circle, these stripes radiate out from the centre. This makes it a great pattern to use with contrasting colours, such as yellow and white. This technique is a stunning and relatively easy one to learn. Once you try this pattern out, you'll want to incorporate it into all your weavings. It's also easy to adjust for any size hoop that you like.

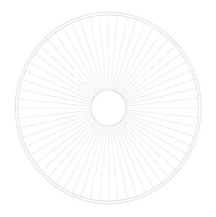

Project dimensions
38cm (15in) in diameter

Note: *If you would like to weave a larger or smaller version of this pattern, the total number of warps must be a multiple of 4. For example, 28, 32, 36 and 52 doubled-up warps would all work for this project.*

SPECIFICATIONS

Open-centre method
(see page 30)

60 doubled-up warps

SUPPLIES

38-cm (15-in) wooden embroidery hoop

5-cm (2in) metal ring

Two bent tapestry needles

Ruler

Clothespin

Scissors

Two to three yarn butterflies made of 100 per cent cotton medium-weight yarn for the warp, roughly 18–27m (20–30yd)

Any yarn in chunky- or super-chunky-weight in two colours for the weft, roughly two 50-m (54-yd) balls

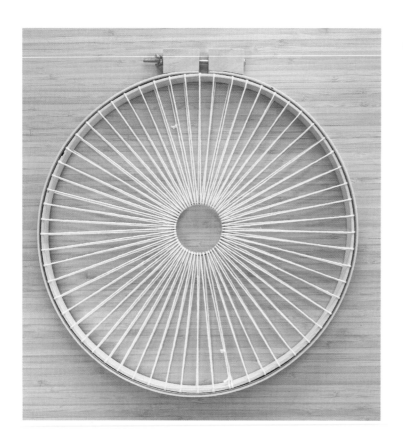

1 Warp the hoop using the open-centre method (see page 30) and 60 doubled-up warps.

2 Once the hoop is set up for open-centre weaving, choose which side will be the front. Next, decide which is to be the main colour (mustard in this example). Measure out 1m (1yd) of yarn. Wrap the centre ring by placing one end of the yarn between two warps. Wrap the yarn around the ring and between the next two warps. Continue wrapping between each warp until you reach the other end.

3 Tie both ends together in a double knot on the backside and trim.

rib weave: over 3, under 1; over 1, under 3

4 Load the bent tapestry needles with 1m (1yd) of each colour. Starting with the dominant colour, begin weaving **over three warps and under one** (see chart, right). Stop weaving before you start the second pass. Pull the yarn to the centre by grasping both ends of yarn and tugging inwards.

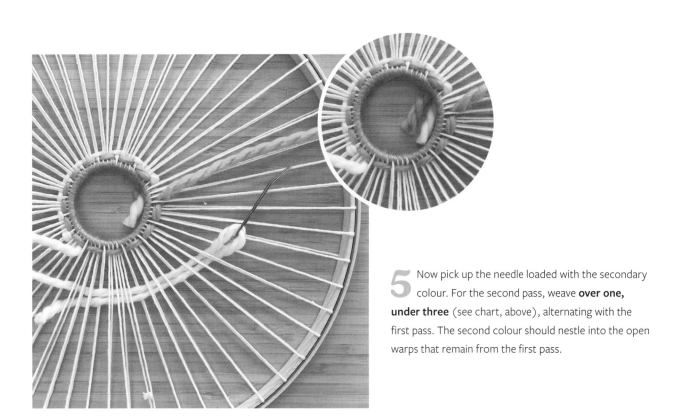

5 Now pick up the needle loaded with the secondary colour. For the second pass, weave **over one, under three** (see chart, above), alternating with the first pass. The second colour should nestle into the open warps that remain from the first pass.

6 Return to the dominant colour and continue weaving **over three, under one** for another pass. Continue alternating the colours on each pass using the same pattern for each colour.

7 When it's time to add more yarn, leave a tail at the back and pull the new yarn through the back to the front. You'll have two tails next to each other on the backside.

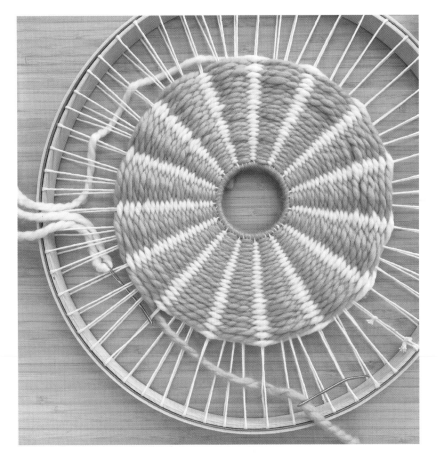

8 Continue weaving the same pattern and alternating colours for each pass to build up the design.

flip it over

9 When you reach the outside edge, flip the weaving over and tie the ends on the back together using a double knot. Choose ends that are next to each other for best results.

10 If you're using an embroidery hoop, place the outer hoop back onto the inner hoop to secure the edges and frame the piece.

‘ **Great job weaving your rib weave wall hanging. This is a great way to add some sunshine to any wall.**’

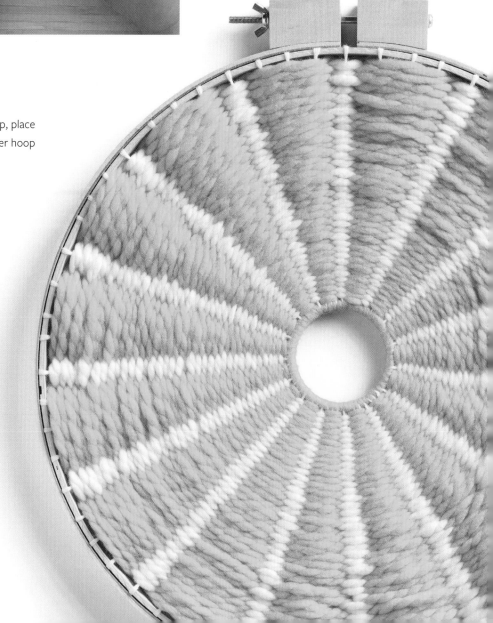

Confetti Inlay Wall Hanging

Do you ever save the ends and remnants of your favourite yarns in the hope of using them one day? If so, this weaving is your opportunity to use them! In this project, you'll create a wall hanging reminiscent of confetti using *inlay*. Inlay is a technique used to add additional patterns, texture or imagery to weavings. There are tons of applications for this, and we're going to start with a quick and straightforward pattern. We'll use short pieces of yarn to 'lay in' extra weft throughout a solid-coloured *tabby* background.

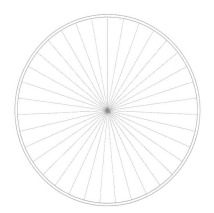

Project dimensions:
20cm (8in) in diameter

Note: *This pattern can be woven on any size of hoop with any odd number of doubled-up warps. You can also choose whether you would prefer an open or closed centre as the design works with both methods.*

SPECIFICATIONS

Closed- or open-centre method (see page 26 or 30)

35 doubled-up warps

SUPPLIES

20-cm (8-in) wooden embroidery hoop

Scissors

Tapestry needle

100 per cent cotton medium-weight yarn for the warp, roughly 60m (65yd)

Chunky- or super-chunky-weight yarn in the same or similar colour as the warp, roughly 50m (54yd)

Scrap yarn in any fibre, weight and colour. Pieces should be around 5–13cm (2–5in) long. You'll need a few handfuls.

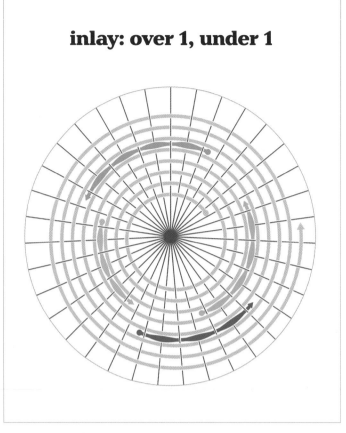

inlay: over 1, under 1

1 Warp the hoop using either the open-centre method (see page 30) or the closed-centre method (see page 26) and 35 doubled-up warps.

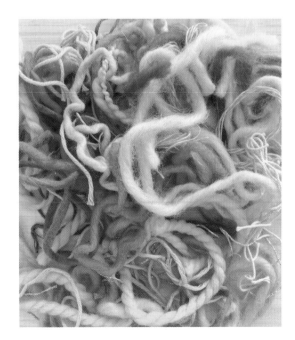

2 If you have a stash of yarn scraps, this is a great opportunity to use them. If not, you can snip pieces of yarn in any colour, fibre or weight. The pieces of yarn should be 5–13cm (2–5in) long. Cut a few handfuls of yarn pieces in as many colours as you choose. You can always cut more pieces if you need them later.

3 Thread the tapestry needle with about 1m (1yd) of chunky yarn for the main weft colour. Begin weaving **over one, under one** (see chart above). This pattern is called tabby weave and we'll use it throughout this project. Because you have an odd number of warps, you'll notice the pattern automatically alternates with each pass. Weave about three passes.

4 Now it's time to lay in the short colourful bits of yarn. Take one of the short pieces of yarn in any colour you like. Using your hands, weave it in using a tabby pattern over and under six to eight warps (see chart opposite). You want to see three to four beads, when the weft is on top of the warp. Tuck the ends behind.

yarn weight

When you start adding in the inlay, use thinner yarns at first. This is recommended because the warps are so close together at the beginning.

5 Pick the needle back up and continue weaving two passes of tabby. You'll notice that the inlayed weft will become sandwiched between the passes. Pack down tightly using the end of the needle.

6 Lay in another short piece of yarn in the same way as in step 4. Do your best to stagger the yarn as shown.

8 As you work your way out from the centre, you can begin adding thicker inlay yarn. You can do this with chunky-weight yarn or by doubling or even tripling up on the thinner yarns, as shown.

7 Continue this pattern of laying in colourful pieces of yarn then weaving a pass or two of the main weft colour.

9 When it's time to add on more chunky-weight weft, tuck the short end to the back. Then measure out a new 1-m (1-yd) long piece, cut, thread the needle and pick up weaving where you left off.

flip it over

10 Keep weaving until your work is 2.5cm (1in) away from the edge of the hoop. Cut a new long piece of main weft yarn. Wrap it around the edge of the hoop starting at one of the warps. Leave a 5-cm (2-in) tail to the backside and wrap the longer end around the hoop, lining up the wraps snugly against each other.

11 When you begin to run out of yarn, tie a second long piece to the tail using a double knot (see page 138). Do your best to position the knot on the back of the hoop by first tying a loose knot and then adjusting it to the right position before tightening. Trim the ends and continue wrapping. Use the same method as before to tie the ends together when you have reached the end.

flip it over

12 Now trim all the hanging ends on the backside of the weaving fairly short, but not so short that they could pull through to the front. As this project will be hung on the wall, trimming the ends should be adequate, but you can tie them together if you prefer.

'Great job weaving your first inlay wall hanging. Feel free to experiment with any colour palette you want. Confetti inlay also looks great with a black backdrop.'

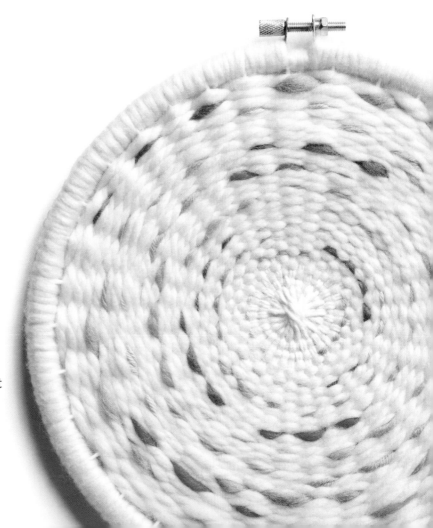

Diamond & Fringe Wall Hanging

In this project, we'll weave radiating triangles and diamonds. This is a technique called *tapestry* where we weave *discontinuous weft*, meaning that instead of weaving in a circle, our weft starts and stops before we've completed a pass. There are endless ways to weave tapestry, but this simple pattern is really effective. We'll emphasize the radiating shapes with a fun fringe made from lark's head knots.

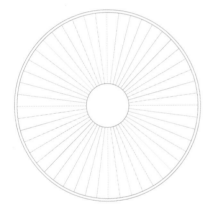

Project dimensions:
30cm (12in) in diameter,
plus fringe

Note: *This pattern can be adjusted for any size hoop. Your total number of doubled-up warps must be divisible by 8. For example 32, 64 or 80 doubled-up warps would work for this project.*

SPECIFICATIONS

Open-centre method
(see page 30)

48 doubled-up warps

SUPPLIES

30-cm (12-in) wooden
embroidery hoop

6-cm (2½-in) fused-metal ring

Scissors

Ruler

Tapestry needle

100 per cent cotton medium-weight yarn for the warp, roughly 6.5m (7yd)

Medium-weight yarn in three colours for the weft, roughly 50m (55yd) each

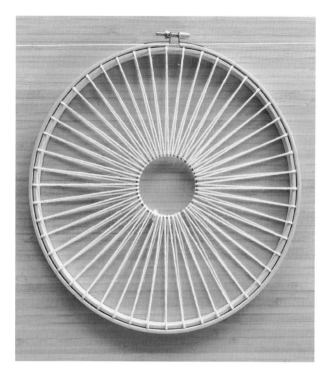

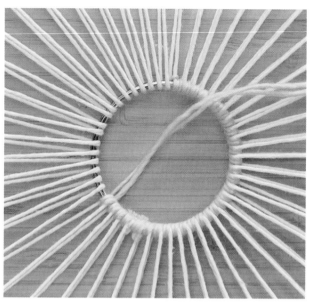

1 Warp the hoop using the open-centre method (see page 30) and 48 doubled-up warps.

2 Measure out about 1.75m (2yd) of yarn in the colour of your choice. Loop the yarn around a warp on the backside to double it. Then wrap the doubled yarn between each set of warps around the centre ring. When you get back to where you started, tie the doubled end to a warp on the back in a double knot. Trim the ends.

4 Then weave your way back. This time make a bubble or hill shape with the weft. Pack it down with the end of the needle to help avoid pulling the warps too closely together.

3 Use a marker, pencil or chalk to mark every eighth warp. You will start the first row of diamonds on the warps you marked. Measure out about 2m (2½ yd) of yarn in the colour of your choice. Loop it around a marked warp. Working anticlockwise, weave one pass of *tabby* **over one warp, under one warp**. Stop before you reach the next marked warp.

5 Weave four passes in this way. Once you've completed these four passes, it's time to reduce one warp on either side to begin narrowing the triangle.

6 Then weave four more passes with one warp fewer on each side. Repeat this process until you have woven four passes on two warps. This is the first triangle. Before you move onto the next triangle, you need to hide the ends. Run the needle along the last warp you wove towards the centre. Pull the needle and yarn through and trim the end. Tuck the ends as you go.

three-colour diamond pattern

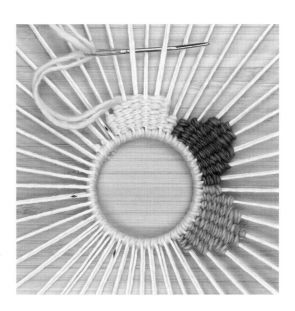

7 Now repeat steps 3–6 for the second coloured triangle. And then the third. Then repeat to add three more triangles. The same colour triangles should be opposite one another in the circle.

8 Once the triangles are complete, it's time to weave a round of diamonds in the gaps. Measure out 4m (4½ yd) of yarn. Loop it around the right warp in the gap between triangles. The first half of the diamond will be like weaving an upside-down triangle. Begin by weaving four passes on two warps. Then four passes on four warps, and so on until you finish weaving four passes on eight warps.

9 Now we're going to reduce one warp on each side to weave four passes on six warps. Then four. Then two. Just like when we wove our first row of triangles. Again, tuck the ends as you go. Repeat this process five more times to complete the round of diamonds.

10 Now let's add some fringe. To prep, cut the yarn into 20-cm (8-in) lengths. You need 192 pieces in each colour, for a total of 576 pieces of yarn.

11 Take two pieces of each colour and make a little bundle for the lark's head knot (see page 139) fringe. Fold all six pieces in half. Place the looped end behind the weaving, with the loop pointing away from the centre. Pull the cut ends up between the warps and thread them through the loop. Pull tight. Once you've tied the first lark's head knot, repeat this with the rest of the yarn. Two bundles should fit between each warp.

12 Once the fringe is attached, brush it out with your fingers or a wide-tooth comb. Flip it over and brush the other side. Then take your time to give it a trim. I start by cutting off the rough ends and then go back and even it out.

fringe finishing

If the fringe seems too floppy, a few light coats of spray starch work great. Just be careful to let it dry between layers.

'Now your wall hanging is ready to hang. There are many ways to incorporate these techniques into other weavings, so I encourage you to explore them for yourself!'

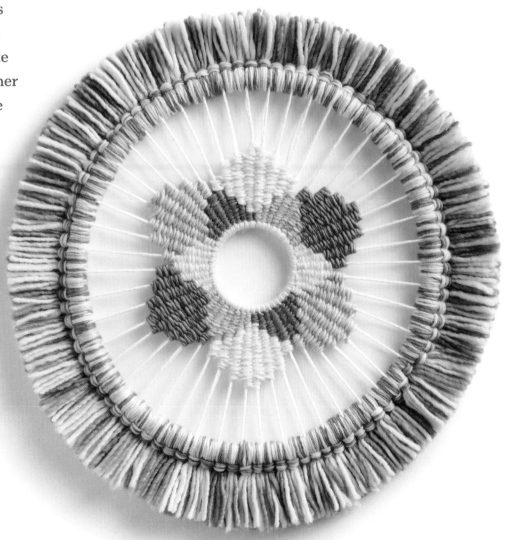

Rya Loop Wall Hanging

In this project, you'll learn how to incorporate a super satisfying raised texture into your weavings through rya loops. You will double, quadruple and octuple medium-weight yarn as you weave out from the centre. I recommend using three colours that are next to each other on the colour wheel for your palette, but feel free to choose any combination of colours you love. Once you learn this technique, you'll want to incorporate it into all of your weavings!

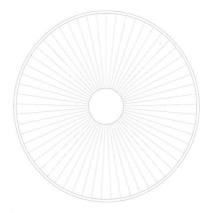

Project dimensions:
30cm (12in) in diameter

Note: *This pattern can be worked with fewer or more warps to create a different look, but the total number of doubled-up warps used must be an odd number.*

SPECIFICATIONS

Open-centre method
(see page 30)

57 doubled-up warps

SUPPLIES

30-cm (12-in) wooden embroidery hoop

6-cm (2½-in) fused-metal ring

Scissors

Ruler

Tapestry needle

100 per cent cotton medium-weight yarn for the warp, roughly 60m (65yd)

Medium-weight yarn in three colours of your choice, roughly 210m (230yd) of each.
I recommend choosing three colours that are next to each other on the colour wheel for visual impact.

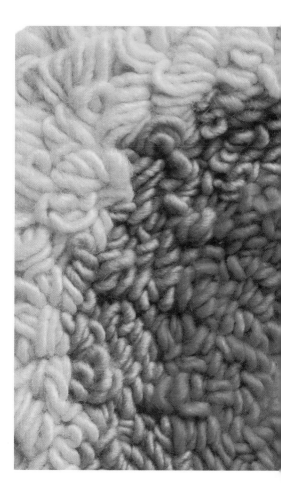

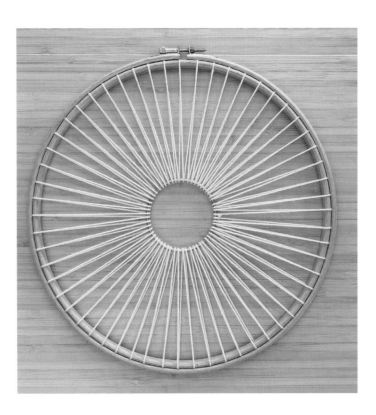

1 Warp the hoop using the open-centre method (see page 30) and 57 doubled-up warps.

2 Measure out 1.75m (2yd) of the first colour you'd like to weave with. Double the length of yarn up and loop it around one of the back warps. Wrap the doubled yarn around the centre ring between each warp. Once you've wrapped the yarn all the way around, tie the ends to the closest warp on the backside using a double knot. Trim the ends.

3 Measure out 1.75m (2yd) of the last colour you will weave with, double the yarn up and loop it onto one of the back warps. Wrap the doubled yarn around the hoop. See page 89 for further instructions on this.

4 Once your outer hoop is wrapped, measure out 1.75m (2yd) of the first colour of yarn and double it up with the looped end on one of the back warps. Working anticlockwise, weave two passes of *tabby* (**over one warp, under one warp**) on doubled-up warps.

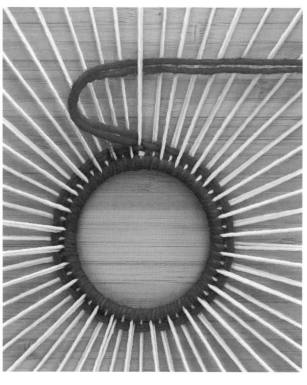

5 Continuing with the same yarn from the first two passes, create a small C-shape underneath the next warp.

6 Fold the C-shape to the right over the top of the right-hand warp, as shown.

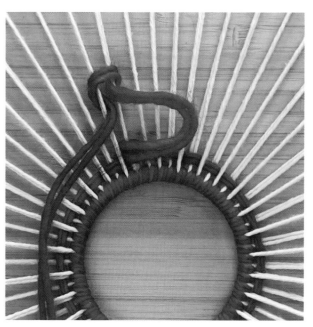

7 Now wrap the yarn behind the warp to the left. Pull through to the front between the two warps.

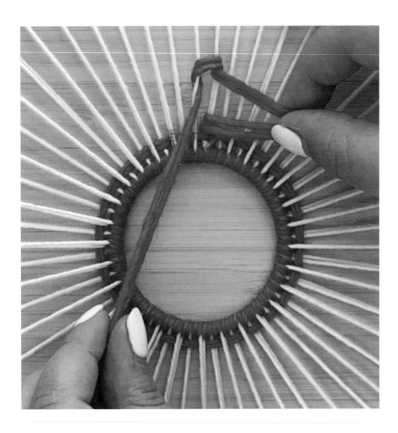

8 Holding the two loops and doubled end of yarn, pull towards the centre. These are your first two rya loops.

9 Working anticlockwise, move to the next two warps and repeat steps 5–8 to create two more rya loops. Continue weaving. When it's time to add on more yarn, bring the cut ends to the front and loop a new piece onto the last warp used, as shown.

10 When you've woven the first pass of rya loops, it's time to weave a second. Because you have an odd number of warps the pattern will automatically alternate so there is no need to change the pattern. Weave the second row of rya loops as before.

11 Now that you've completed the first two rows of rya loops, you need to secure them. Weave two rows of tabby (**over one warp, under one warp**) and pack down tightly with the end of the needle. Continue weaving this pattern of two rows of rya loops followed by two rows of tabby weave.

12 Stop weaving when the first colour covers about a third of the distance between the centre ring and outer hoop. Flip over to measure on the backside as it will be more difficult to take an accurate measurement with all the volume on the front.

13 Repeat the same pattern with the second yarn colour. This time, quadruple the strands of yarn so you end up with four rya loops at a time. Weave this section until you are two thirds of the way to the outer hoop.

14 Repeat the same pattern with the third yarn colour. This time, octuple the yarn so you end up with eight rya loops at a time. This will help compensate for the greater distance between the warps.

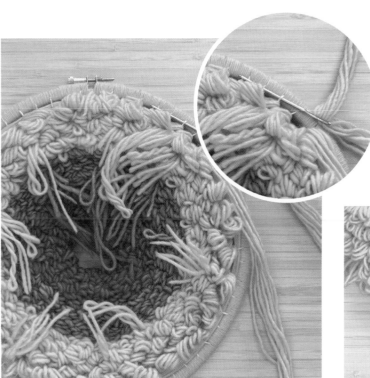

15 When the warp becomes too tight to add more rya loops, weave tabby in the third colour to the outer edge of the hoop.

16 Now that you've finished weaving, trim the ends to a similar length as the rya loops. There is no need to tuck or tie the ends for this project as they blend in with the loops.

'Your Rya Loop Wall Hanging is now complete! Now that you've learned this technique, I recommend incorporating it into your other weavings for added texture.'

Leno Wall Hanging

In this project, you will use two colours and a technique called *leno* to create a totally different kind of circular weaving! We'll weave circles that highlight the warp through negative space. Leno is a type of weaving referred to as *hand-manipulated lace*, which means that you will use your needle to twist the warps as you weave in the weft. These twists will be suspended between layers of tabby weave for an open and airy design.

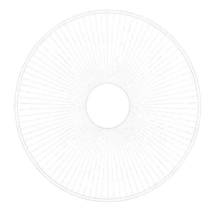

Project dimensions:
25cm (10in) in diameter

Note: *This pattern can be woven on any size of hoop – I used a 25-cm (10-in) wooden embroidery hoop and a 5-cm (2-in) fused-metal ring. To create this design, you need an even number of individual warps with an open centre.*

SPECIFICATIONS

Open-centre method
(see page 30)

90 individual warps

SUPPLIES

25-cm (10-in) wooden
embroidery hoop

5-cm (2-in) fused-metal ring

Scissors

Sewing needle with a large eye

Tapestry needle

100 per cent cotton medium-weight yarn in the colour of your choice, roughly 60m (65yd)

Sparkly super-fine-weight yarn, roughly 25m (27yd) (two skeins of embroidery silks would also work)

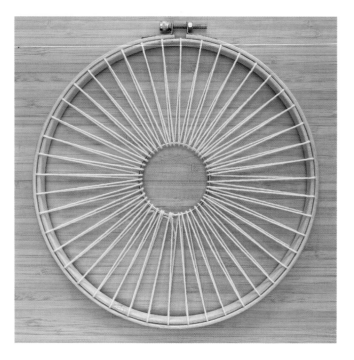

1 Warp the hoop using the open-centre method (see page 30) and 90 individual warps. Attach the outer hoop to secure the warp edges.

2 Measure out about 1.75m (2yd) of yarn and wrap the centre ring in the same yarn you used for the warp. Tie the ends together on the backside using a double knot (see page 138). Trim the ends.

3 Measure out about 1.75m (2yd) of sparkly yarn and double it up. Thread the centre loop around a single warp on the backside, as shown. Flip the hoop over with the front side up and begin wrapping the yarn around the outer hoop keeping the wraps next to each other, not overlapping.

yarn selection

I suggest choosing one sparkly thread-weight yarn and an Aran-weight yarn to complement one another. The sparkly yarn goes well with the delicate openness of this pattern.

4 Continue wrapping the outer hoop. When you reach the tension hook on the embroidery hoop, use a needle to help pull the yarn through and around the hook.

5 When you run out of sparkly yarn, measure out another piece then tie the four cut ends (two from the old piece, two from the new) together using a loose knot. The knot needs to be positioned on the backside of the hoop. This can be tricky so be sure to leave the yarn end a little longer in case you need to adjust. Once the knot is in place, tighten and continue wrapping with the new yarn over the top of the ends to hide them.

6 You'll probably need to add on new yarn a few times because the thread weight is so thin. When you come to a looped end, instead of tying the ends together as in step 5, simply loop the new yarn through the old yarn, as shown. Then keep wrapping.

7 Once you've wrapped the whole of the outer hoop, tie the yarn that you've been wrapping with onto a single warp on the backside. Double knot it and use a sewing needle to tuck the ends underneath where you wrapped. Trim the ends.

8 Now that the hoop is wrapped, we finally get to start weaving! Thread a tapestry needle with about 1m (1yd) of Aran-weight yarn and weave a pass of *tabby* anticlockwise, working **over one, under one** on individual warps. Weave over each front warp and under each back warp to ensure that the front warp is on the right and back warp is on the left, as shown.

9 When you've finished the first pass, you'll notice that the pattern doesn't automatically alternate. This is because we need an even number of warps for the leno weave. This means you'll need to consciously adjust the pattern at the end of each pass. The fun part is that you'll get to weave through the shed with every other pass. That means that you can slide the needle through the open warps instead of weaving up and down.

10 Weave four passes of tabby in total. On the backside, tie the ends together in a double knot (see page 138) and trim.

leno

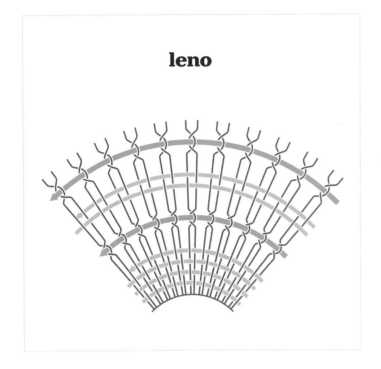

11 Now it's time to weave the leno. Measure out 1m (1yd) of sparkly yarn, double it up and loop it around a back warp. Working anticlockwise, use the tip of the needle to pull the back warp up and to the right of the top warp, as shown. Do this a few times before pulling the weft through. Make sure the warp that is holding the loop isn't pulled too far to the left.

12 Continue to weave a pass of leno with the sparkly yarn. To connect the start and end of the pass, run the needle along the two starting twists and tie a small double knot onto the backside. Trim the end.

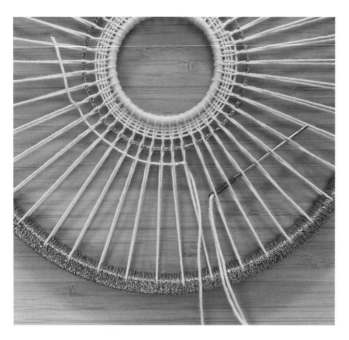

14 When the two passes are complete, tie the ends together on the backside and trim.

13 To suspend the twist, weave two passes of tabby as in step 8, ensuring the front warp is on the right and back warp is on the left, as shown.

15 Continue alternating one pass of leno with two passes of tabby.

using leno

After you've completed this project, I highly recommend playing with how to incorporate it into other weavings with an even number of warps. Leno is a lovely way to add lightness to any weaving!

16 Keep going until the warps feel too tight to continue weaving. You don't want the hoop to bend so it's a good idea to leave plenty of open warps.

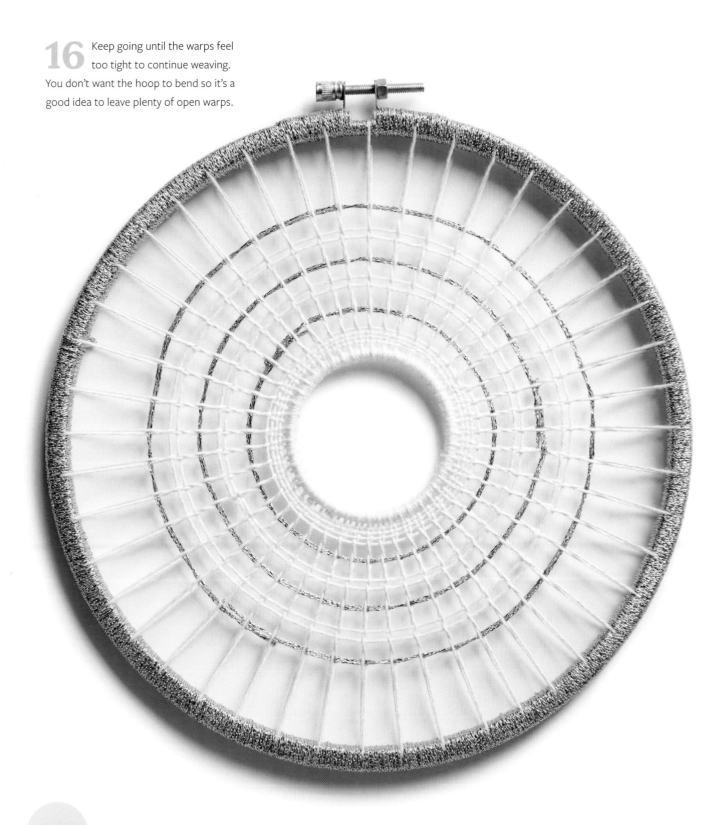

'I hope you enjoyed creating this delicate lace-like wall hanging. These weavings look great hung on a wall or a window to show off the beautiful pattern.'

Twisted Warps Wall Hanging

In this project, we explore the third method of warping a hoop, mentioned on page 22. This involves attaching individual lengths of yarn to a centre ring using lark's head knots and then tying the cut ends in a bow at the outer hoop. Although this process takes a little longer than the open and closed-centre warping methods, this technique allows you to twist individually woven sections, creating spirals that radiate from the centre to the outer edge. I hope you enjoy this advanced woven wall hanging!

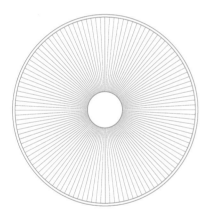

Project dimensions:
30cm (12in) in diameter

Note: *It is not recommended to adjust the total number of individual warps for this project due to the pattern used.*

SPECIFICATIONS

Open-centre method
(see page 30)

120 individual warps

SUPPLIES

30-cm (12-in) wooden embroidery hoop

6-cm (2½-in) fused metal-ring

Scissors

Ruler

Tapestry needle

Thin tapestry needle with a large eye

100 per cent cotton medium-weight yarn in two colours for both warp and weft, roughly 55m (60yd) each

1 Take both colours of yarn and cut thirty pieces of each. Each length should be about 46cm (18in) long for a 30-cm (12-in) embroidery hoop.

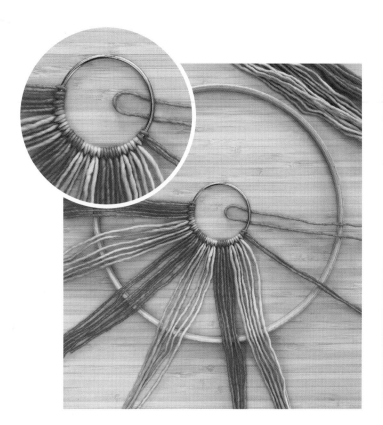

2 Remove the outer hoop from the embroidery hoop and set to the side. Centre the fused metal ring at the centre of the inner hoop. Now tie each length of yarn to the centre ring using a lark's head knot. Alternate three knots in the primary colour (I chose pink), then three in the secondary colour (beige). You will have six individual warps per section.

3 Imagine your weaving is a clock, and take two individual warps from numbers 12, 3, 6 and 9. Tie these warps to the outer hoop as if they were supplemental ties (see page 31). Use a bow instead of a double knot as you will need to untie these later. For each tie, make sure to keep the individual warp on the left up, and the warp on the right down. This is to keep the warps organized when you start weaving.

4 Now work on tying the remaining warps to the hoop. First tie the warps on either side of the first bow. Then tie the same two warps on the opposite side. Repeat this pattern of tying a few bows on each side until you have tied all the warps onto the hoop. Alternating in this way will help keep the ring centred. Once all the bows are tied, space the warps evenly around the hoop.

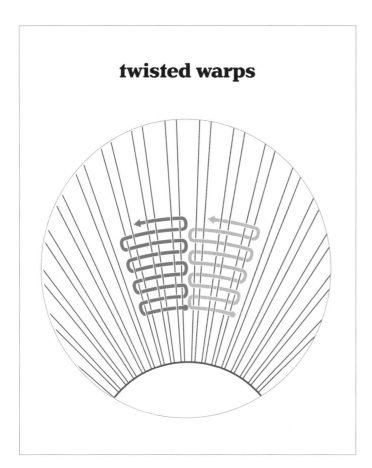

twisted warps

5 Now it's time to begin weaving. Instead of weaving round and round the centre like most of the projects in this book, we will weave each coloured section separately. Thread a tapestry needle with about 1m (1yd) of Aran-weight yarn in the primary colour and weave *tabby* (**over one, under one**) on the six individual warps that correspond to that colour (see chart, left). To keep the edges of the sections from pulling inwards, create a small bubble or hill shape with the weft for each pass. Then pack the bubble down with the end of the needle. This will help to keep the edges straighter.

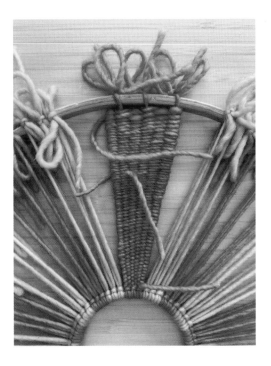

6 If you need to add on more yarn in a section, leave one end to the back and one to the front. Continue weaving each primary-coloured section.

7 Now that you've finished weaving the first set of sections, tuck the ends in using a small tapestry needle and trim any excess yarn. This includes any ends where you added on more yarn.

8 Now it's time to weave the other sections in the secondary colour. Move the warps closer together than in the first sections. Thread a tapestry needle with 1m (1yd) of Aran-weight yarn in the secondary colour. This time, instead of weaving individual warps, we will weave these sections on doubled-up warps. Now begin weaving on the three doubled-up warps using tabby weave. These sections will be much narrower than the first ones you wove. When you're done weaving each section in this way, tuck the ends in and trim the excess yarn.

9 Now it's time to twist! Starting with the primary-coloured sections, untie the bows for one section. Twist this section once to the left. Retie the ends onto the hoop using double knots (see page 138) and trim the ends.

10 Repeat for the section on the opposite side of the hoop. Continue this pattern until you've twisted and tied off all the primary sections.

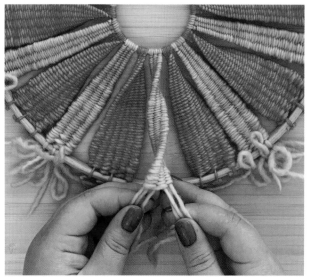

11 Now it's time to twist the secondary sections. Untie one section at a time and twist to the left twice. Retie the ends onto the hoop using double knots and trim the ends. Repeat for the section on the opposite side of the hoop and continue this pattern for each remaining section.

12 Now that each section is twisted, place the outer hoop back onto the inner hoop. Wrap both hoops in the colour of your choice. I recommend doubling up the yarn for speed and to ensure good coverage. See page 89 for detailed instructions on this.

'That's it! Now your Twisted Warps Wall Hanging is finished and ready to hang. I hope you enjoyed learning this third way to warp a hoop!'

Cloud Inlay Wall Hanging

In this project, you'll learn how to weave puffy clouds using a technique called *inlay*. If this is your first time weaving inlay, I recommend completing the Confetti Inlay Wall Hanging on page 84 first. This pattern is a bit more advanced as it requires an understanding of how inlay unfolds and some intuition for the shape and positioning of the clouds.

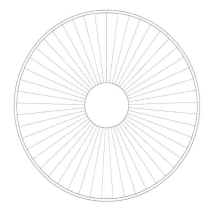

Project dimensions:
20cm (8in) in diameter

Note: *This pattern can be woven on any size of hoop with any odd number of doubled-up warps.*

SPECIFICATIONS

Open-centre method
(see page 30)

49 doubled-up warps

SUPPLIES

20-cm (8-in) wooden embroidery hoop

5-cm (2-in) fused-metal ring

Scissors

Tapestry needle

100 per cent cotton light-weight yarn in blue or the colour of your choice for the warp and main weft, roughly 125m (137yd)

Super-chunky-weight yarn in white or the colour of your choice for the clouds, roughly 4.5m (5yd)

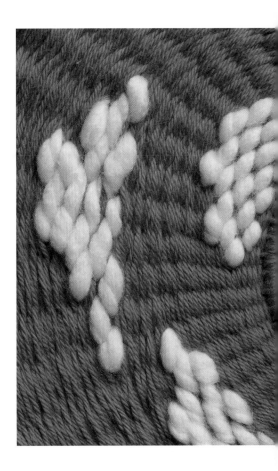

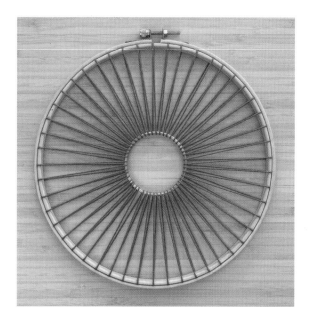

1 Warp the hoop using the open-centre method (see page 30) and 49 doubled-up warps. I recommend using the same colour yarn for the warp as you will for the main weft colour as this will create a clean backdrop for the clouds.

2 Measure out about 1.75m (2yd) of yarn using the same yarn you used for the warp. As this yarn is quite thin, I suggest looping the length of yarn to one of the back warps to double it up. Wrap the doubled yarn between each warp. When you've reached where you started, tie the ends to the closest back warp in a double knot. Trim the ends.

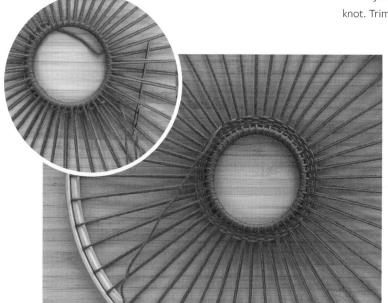

3 The main weaving for this project is *tabby* weave. Load the tapestry needle with about 1m (1yd) of the same yarn you used for the warp. Begin weaving **over one, under one**. Stop when you have completed about five passes around the centre. Pull the remaining yarn and needle to the back. We'll pick up weaving with the needle later.

4 Now let's begin weaving the inlay. Cut two pieces of super-chunky-weight yarn in white or the colour of your choice to about 46cm (18in). A needle is not necessary as we'll only be weaving small sections.

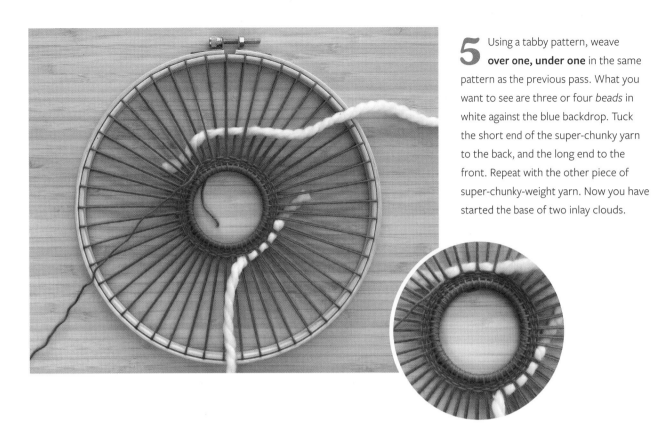

5 Using a tabby pattern, weave **over one, under one** in the same pattern as the previous pass. What you want to see are three or four *beads* in white against the blue backdrop. Tuck the short end of the super-chunky yarn to the back, and the long end to the front. Repeat with the other piece of super-chunky-weight yarn. Now you have started the base of two inlay clouds.

6 Now pick up the needle loaded with blue yarn and weave three passes on top of the first layer of inlay, alternating the pattern from the last pass of blue yarn. Be sure to pack the yarn down and don't be afraid to weave tightly. If you find the super-chunky yarn is getting in the way, it may be helpful to thread the long ends through the open centre.

inlay cloud patterns

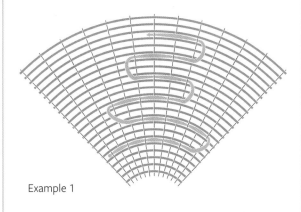

Example 1

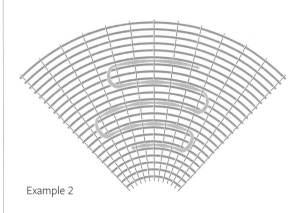

Example 2

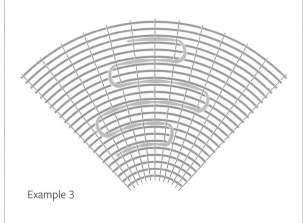

Example 3

7 Now it's time to weave the second pass of inlay for the first two clouds. Again you'll want to match the **over one, under one** pattern to that of the last pass. Essentially, you'll create the puffy clouds using a zigzag-like pattern with the super-chunky yarn. There are some pattern examples in the charts, left, but this is a great time to practise weaving intuitively to see what you come up with!

8 Weave three passes in blue and pack down tightly. You'll notice that because you wove an odd number of passes between the first and second pass of inlay, the beads will be in the alternate gaps as the first pass. This is what creates the puffy cloud shape rather than vertical stripes.

9 Continue this pattern of weaving one pass of inlay between three passes of blue. Once you're about halfway through the first two clouds, follow the instructions as before to begin another cloud, as shown. Or feel free to wait until you've completed the first two clouds. Either way, it's best practice to keep all of the inlay weaving in the same pass so you can continue the same rhythm of three passes of blue and one pass of inlay.

10 Keep going! As the weaving progresses, add in more clouds in the gaps between the clouds. You can add one, two or three clouds at a time. It is easy to unweave if you feel your design isn't looking right.

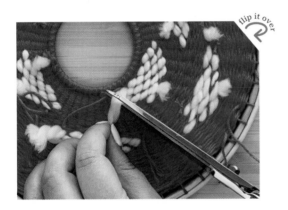

flip it over

' Great job weaving clouds using inlay. If you want to continue practising this technique, feel free to experiment weaving inlay of different shapes and symbols. The options are endless!'

11 When you begin to run out of yarn, tie a second long piece to the tail using a double knot (see page 138), positioned on the back of the hoop. Trim the ends and continue wrapping. Use the same method as before to tie the ends together when you have reached the end.

12 Place the outer hoop back onto the inner hoop to secure the edges and frame the piece.

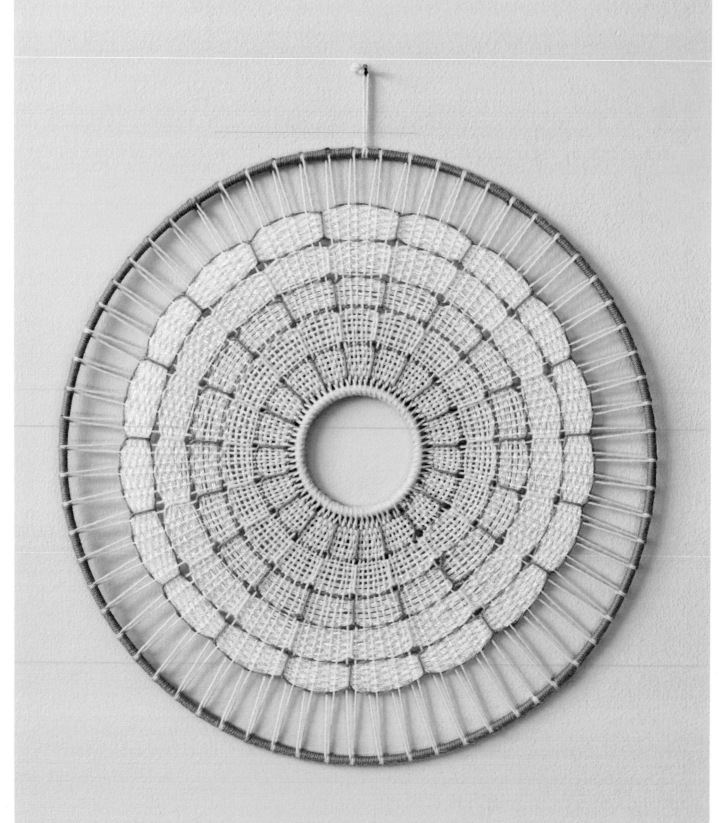

Danish Medallion Wall Hanging

This delicate wall hanging uses a hand-manipulated lace technique called *Danish medallions*. Although mostly tabby weave, we'll wrap the weft in a way that creates individual sections or medallions that encircle the centre ring. The open design of this project works well with a sparkly yarn, but this is not essential.

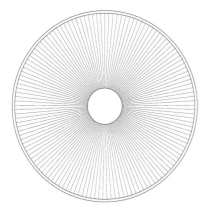

Project dimensions:
30cm (12in) in diameter

Note: *This pattern can be worked with fewer or more warps to create a different look, but the total number of individual warps used must be a multiple of 7.*

SPECIFICATIONS

Open-centre method
(see page 30)

133 individual warps

SUPPLIES

30-cm (12-in) metal hoop

6-cm (2½-in) fused-metal ring

Scissors

Clear tape

Two extra-long tapestry needles, about 13cm (5in) long (if you can't find these then any tapestry needles will work fine)

Ruler

100 per cent cotton light-weight yarn in two colours for the warp and weft, roughly 40m (45yd) each

Sparkly super-fine-weight yarn for the weft, roughly 45m (50yd)

1 Warp the hoop using the open-centre method (see page 30) and 133 individual warps. Choose either colour of cotton for the warp (I chose lavender). This will be the primary colour.

single warp

Because there is an odd number of individual warps in this design, there will be a single warp tied onto the outer edge.

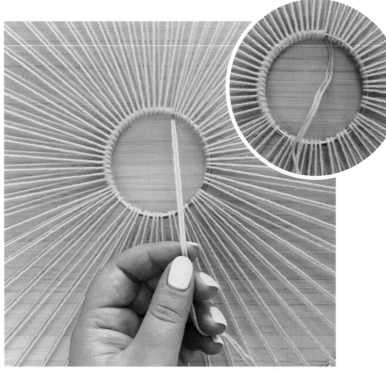

2 Using the primary colour, double up about 1m (1yd) of yarn and loop it onto one of the back warps. Then wrap the doubled-up strand of yarn between each warp around the centre ring. When you've wrapped all the way around, tie the remaining yarn to one of the back warps and trim the ends.

3 Using the secondary colour (I chose purple), double up about 1m (1yd) of yarn and loop onto one of the back warps. Begin wrapping the doubled-up yarn around the outer hoop.

4 When the secondary yarn runs low, stop just before a warp and use a small piece of clear tape to affix the end to the hoop. Trim the end poking out of the tape. Measure out a new piece of yarn as before and loop it onto the back of the warp where you stopped wrapping. Continue wrapping. Repeat as many times as needed until you reach where you started. Tie the ends onto the last warp on the backside and trim the ends.

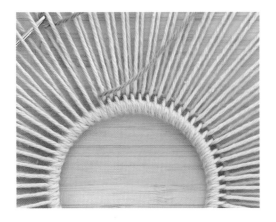

5 Now that the outer and inner hoops are both wrapped, it's time to start weaving. Thread the tapestry needle with 1m (1yd) of the secondary yarn colour and weave one pass of *tabby* (**over one, under one**) around the centre using individual warps. Tuck both the short and long ends to the back.

weft gapping

Don't worry if you see open space between passes of weft. This happens when the warps are very close together. The space between the weft will change as you work your way out.

6 Double up 1m (1yd) of sparkly yarn and loop it around the next warp. This is called the filler yarn. Thread the second tapestry needle with both ends of the filler yarn and continue weaving tabby until you have about 1cm (½in) of weaving.

7 Now we'll begin wrapping our weft to create our first medallion. Pick up the needle threaded with the secondary colour. Start weaving another pass of tabby, but only over and under seven warps. When you reach the seventh warp, bring the needle to the back of the weaving. Pull your needle back to the front between the first pass and centre ring, and between the seventh and eighth warps. This will create a vertical line of yarn on the backside of your weaving.

8 Now thread the needle through the last bead you wove on the top part of the medallion, as shown.

9 Pull down to tighten, then up to prepare for your next medallion. Now you have a vertical line of yarn on the frontside too. This is the start of your first medallion! You'll weave the other vertical line to complete the medallion at the end of this row.

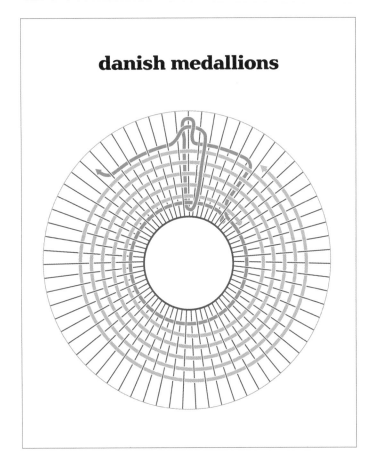

danish medallions

10 Weave over and under the next seven warps, then repeat steps 7, 8 and 9 to create the second medallion.

repeating pattern

You'll repeat this pattern every seven warps to create nine medallions around the centre ring. Double and triple check that there are seven warps in each medallion before proceeding. Subsequent rows of medallions will be quicker to create as you will be able to follow the pattern from the first round.

11 When it's time to add on more yarn, it's best to do this in the middle of a medallion. It will be less noticeable this way. Flip the weaving over and tie the ends together on the back. For this project, I recommend tying ends as you go rather than saving them for the end.

12 When you've completed the last medallion, tie the ends of the secondary yarn together on the backside. If you have sparkly yarn remaining, there is no need to trim it as you can continue with the same strand later.

13 Now it's time to start the second row of medallions. Weave one pass of tabby in the primary colour. Then weave 1cm (½in) of filler yarn as in step 6. Then switch back to the primary colour to complete the medallions as described in steps 7, 8 and 9. Continue alternating the primary and secondary colours around the filler yarn with each row.

14 When the warps feel too tight to weave another row of medallions, stop. Tuck or tie any remaining ends on the backside.

'Using a small piece of yarn, tie the ends together in a double knot. Then attach it to the top of the circle using a lark's head knot (see page 139). Now you're ready to hang your Danish Medallions Wall Hanging!'

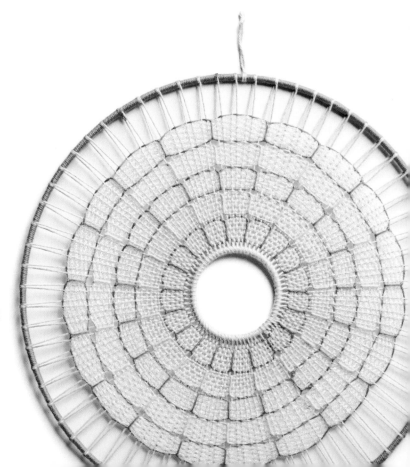

Crescent Moon Wall Hanging

In this project, we'll cover a slight variation of setting up an open-centre warp by attaching the centre ring to the outer hoop. Instead of weaving around the centre, we'll weave back and forth to create a radiating backdrop for a crescent moon shape. Once you complete this project, there are endless ways to use these techniques. I recommend that you complete the Sunny Rib Weave Wall Hanging (page 78) and Diamond & Fringe Wall Hanging (page 90) before beginning this project.

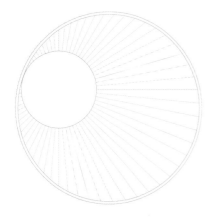

Project dimensions:
30cm (12in) in diameter

Note: *This pattern can be worked with fewer or more warps to create a different look, but the number of doubled-up warps used must be a multiple of 4.*

SPECIFICATIONS

Open-centre method
(see page 30)

68 doubled-up warps

SUPPLIES

30-cm (12-in) metal hoop

13-cm (5-in) fused-metal ring

Scissors

Ruler

Three tapestry needles

100 per cent cotton medium-weight yarn for the warp, roughly 11m (12yd)

Chunky-weight yarn in three colours and the fibre of your choice for the weft, roughly 18m (20yd) of each colour

1 Place the smaller ring at the inside edge of the larger ring. Measure out about 3.5m (4yd) of chunky-weight yarn in the colour of your choice (I used white). With a tail to one side, begin wrapping the yarn around both hoops in a figure-eight pattern. Pull to bring the ring and hoop together, just tight enough that it feels secure. Continue wrapping in a figure-eight motion for about 5cm (2in).

2 Once the rings are connected, begin wrapping the same yarn around the larger hoop. Keep the wraps close enough that you completely cover the hoop beneath. When you reach the other side, wrap the yarn underneath the smaller hoop towards the centre.

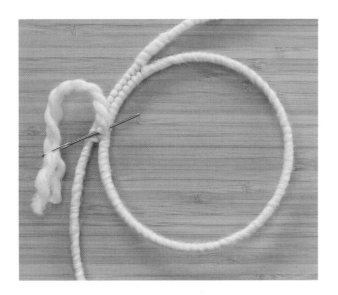

3 Now it's time to wrap the smaller hoop. Wrap the yarn around in the same way as for the outer hoop. When the smaller hoop is completely covered, use a tapestry needle to tuck the end under the figure-eight wraps on the backside and tie the two ends together in a double knot (see page 138). Trim the ends.

off-centre rings

If you enjoy the off-centre look, feel free to experiment with combining it with other techniques. There are endless ways to utilize this set up beyond this project!

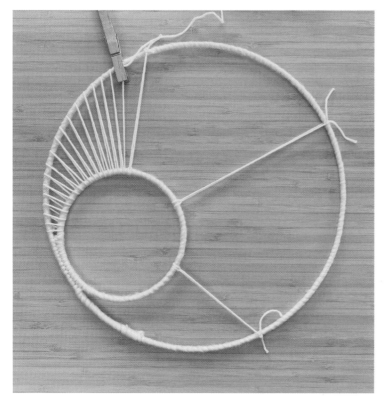

4 Now that the hoops are wrapped, it will be easier to warp the otherwise slippery hoops. Tie three supplemental ties from the inner hoop to the outer hoop (see page 31). Now tie the warp yarn onto the outer hoop and begin warping as for the open-centre method (see page 30) for a total of 68 doubled-up warps.

5 Thread two tapestry needles with about 1m (1yd) of two colours of the chunky-weight yarn. Take the first colour (I chose navy) and begin weaving **over three, under one** to start the *rib weave* backdrop of the moon. Stop when you reach the other side. Pick up the other needle (I chose sea foam) and starting on the same side as the first pass, begin weaving **under three, over one**.

6 Now you need to work back the other way. Pick up your first needle and weave **over three, under one,** just like you did before. Then follow with the second needle, weaving **over one, under three**. As you work your way back and forth in this pattern, you'll need to reduce the number of warps you weave as you meet the outer hoop.

flip it over

7 When you need to add on more weft, simply leave a tail to the backside, cut a new piece of yarn, and pick up where you left off.

8 Continue until your weaving measures about 4cm (1½in) from the centre ring.

9 Now it's time to weave the crescent moon. Thread another tapestry needle with about 1m (1yd) of the third colour of chunky-weight yarn (I chose white). Weave one pass of tabby (**over one, under one**) across all the open warps. Then turn around and weave a second pass back across all the open warps to create the base of the moon. Now continue weaving back and forth, reducing by four warps on either side on each pass.

10 When you can't reduce another four warps on each side, it's time to smooth out the step pattern that you'll notice has emerged from reducing warps with each pass. Weave all the way to one side, and then back to the other. This pass-and- a-half of tabby will finish the moon with a clean rounded edge.

flip it over

12 Continue weaving in rib as in steps 5–6 until you reach the edge of the hoop. Once the rib weave is finished, flip the weaving over and tie and tuck in any loose weft ends. Trim as needed.

11 Now pick up where you left off with the rib weave pattern. Be careful not to switch up the pattern when you resume. Because of this break in the pattern, you'll notice that the warps are much farther apart now.

'Now cut a small piece of yarn and attach it to the top of the outer hoop using a lark's head knot (see page 139). Tie the cut ends in an overhand knot. Now you're ready to hang your Crescent Moon Wall Hanging.'

Glossary

Definitions throughout the glossary relate specifically to circular weaving.

Bead
The front-facing weft that is visible between each warp. Like a photo is made up of pixels, weaving is made up of beads.

Danish medallions
A hand-manipulated lace technique where the top and bottom passes of weft are wrapped around filler weft to create individual cells or medallions.

Discontinuous weft
Weft that stops before completing a full pass around the centre of the circular weaving. It is often used to add additional colours or shapes to a weaving.

Double cloth
A technique in which two or more sets of warps are woven separately and/or together to create layers of cloth. Also called 'double weave'.

Hand-manipulated lace
A lace-like cloth woven on a loom. Refers to a subset of weaving that includes techniques like Danish medallions, leno, Brooks bouquet and many more.

Inlay
A weaving technique where additional weft is added into a pass to add texture, colour or pictorial effect.

Leno
A hand-manipulated lace technique where the warp is twisted between passes of tabby weave. The twists are secured with weft to create lace-like cloth.

Loom
A device or frame used to weave cloth. Its main function is to keep warps under tension during the weaving process.

Pass
When the weft makes a complete circle around the centre. Or when weft is woven from the designated start to the stop point in tapestry weaving.

Rib weave
A form of tabby weave that uses two or more colours to create radiating stripes or ribs of colour. The pattern is often reversed on the backside.

Shed
When weaving on individual warps, the shed is the natural space between the top and bottom warps created by the edge of the hoop.

Shuttle
A tool used to guide weft over and under the appropriate warps. In circular weaving, this is often some kind of needle.

Soumak
A technique where the weft wraps around the warps. When two passes are woven in opposite directions on top of each other, it creates a braid-like effect in the weaving.

Supplemental ties
Additional yarn used to temporarily suspend a ring in the centre of a hoop for open-centre weaving. These ties are later removed as the hoop is warped.

Tabby
Also called plain weave. The simplest and most common weaving pattern where the weft goes over one warp, under one warp.

Tapestry
A style of weaving that uses discontinuous weft to create shapes and pictures in the cloth.

Tension
When the warp is stretched tight across the loom to create a rigid foundation for the weft to be woven through.

Twill
A weaving technique that creates a swirling effect around the centre of the weaving.

Warp
Yarn that is stretched across the loom, like the skeleton of a weaving.

Weft
Yarn that is woven over and under the warp to create the cloth.

Yarn butterfly
A method of bundling yarn for easier handling.

Yarns Used by Project

Paintbox Yarns Cotton Aran, MillaMia Naturally Soft Super Chunky, Malabrigo Chunky, Malabrigo Worsted and Anchor Artiste Metallic yarns were kindly provided by LoveCrafts.

Twill Woven Bunting (page 36)
Weft: Paintbox Yarns Cotton Aran in Washed Teal
Warp: Malabrigo Worsted Merino Wool in Tuareg, Water Green and Natural

Striped Tabby Pillow (page 42)
Weft: Paintbox Yarns Cotton Aran in Paper White
Warp: Malabrigo Chunky Merino Wool in Applewood, Burgundy, Rhodesian and Frank Ochre

Tabby Weave Rag Rug (page 50)
Weft: Paintbox Yarns Cotton Aran in Paper White
Warp: Cotton fabric

Swirly Twill Coasters (page 56)
Weft: Paintbox Yarns Cotton Aran in Paper White
Warp: Paintbox Yarns Cotton Aran in Melon Sorbet

Double Cloth Soumak Pillow (page 62)
Weft: Paintbox Yarns Cotton Aran in Paper White
Warp: Malabrigo Worsted Merino Wool in Tuareg, Water Green, Sunset, Sauterne and Natural

Circular Placemats (page 70)
Weft: Paintbox Yarns Cotton Aran in Paper White
Warp: Malabrigo Chunky Merino Wool in Applewood and Rhodesian; Malabrigo Worsted Merino Wool in Natural

Sunny Rib Weave Wall Hanging (page 78)
Weft: Paintbox Yarns Cotton Aran in Paper White
Warp: MillaMia Naturally Soft Super Chunky in Cream and Sunshine

Confetti Inlay Wall Hanging (page 84)
Weft: Paintbox Yarns Cotton Aran in Paper White
Warp: MillaMia Naturally Soft Super Chunky in Cream; various scraps and fibres

Diamond & Fringe Wall Hanging (page 90)
Weft: Paintbox Yarns Cotton Aran in Paper White
Warp: Malabrigo Worsted Merino Wool in Natural, Water Green, and Lettuce

Rya Loop Wall Hanging (page 96)
Weft: Paintbox Yarns Cotton Aran in Paper White
Warp: Malabrigo Worsted Merino Wool in Glazed Carrots, Sunset, and Sauterne

Leno Wall Hanging (page 104)
Weft: Paintbox Yarns Cotton Aran in Paper White
Warp: Anchor Artiste Metallic Thread Weight in Gold

Twisted Warps Wall Hanging (page 112)
Weft and Warp: Malabrigo Worsted Merino Wool in Cactus Flower and Pale Khaki

Cloud Inlay Wall Hanging (page 118)
Weft: Paintbox Yarns Cotton Aran in Marine Blue
Warp: Paintbox Yarns Cotton Aran in Marine Blue; MillaMia Naturally Soft Super Chunky in Cream

Danish Medallion Wall Hanging (page 124)
Weft: Paintbox Yarns Cotton Aran in Dusty Rose
Warp: Anchor Artiste Metallic Thread Weight in White; Paintbox Yarns Cotton Aran in Tea Rose

Crescent Moon Wall Hanging (page 130)
Weft: Paintbox Yarns Cotton Aran in Paper White
Warp: MillaMia Naturally Soft Super Chunky in Cream, Sailor Blue and Eau De Nil

Knots

The following knots are used in various projects thoughout the book.

Double half hitch

Often used to secure weft before removing a weaving from the loom.

1 Using a long continuous piece of yarn, wrap one end over the top of a warp. Thread the end between the wrap and the edge of the weaving as you bring it to the front. This is the first half hitch.

2 Repeat this same wrapping motion from on top of the first half hitch. Pull to tighten your double half hitch. Move to the next warp and repeat both steps.

Double Knot

Often used when securing supplemental ties for open-centre weaving, or when tying ends together on the backside of a weaving.

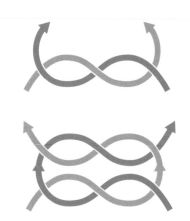

1 Cross two ends of yarn with one end on top and the other behind. Fold the top yarn down and behind both ends. Then lead this end back up. This will cause both pieces of yarn to twist together.

2 Cross both ends again. Fold top end down and to the back. Then thread the end through the opening and pull tight. Trim ends as needed.

Overhand Knot

Often used when securing the first supplemental tie for open-centre weaving, or when attaching a new yarn butterfly to an existing one.

1 Hold two ends of yarn together. Create a circle with both ends by folding and crossing the cut ends over the lengths of yarn.

2 Then thread the two ends through the circle. Pull to tighten. Trim ends as needed.

Lark's Head Knot

Often used to attach supplemental ties to the centre ring for open-centre weaving or to add fringe to the edge of a weaving. Can be used with one or several pieces of yarn.

1 Fold your yarn in half. Place the looped end underneath whatever you're tying your knot onto.

2 Then take the two ends and thread them through the looped end. Pull to tighten.

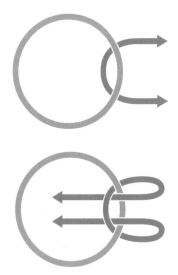

Cow Hitch

Similar to a lark's head knot but tied using a continuous length of yarn instead of a predetermined length of yarn.

1 Starting from behind the hoop or whatever you're tying your knot onto, take the end of a piece of yarn and loop it over and behind itself.

2 Now bring that end down and across the front.

3 Thread the end from behind to the front through the opening. Pull to tighten.

Templates

Cardboard Loom Template

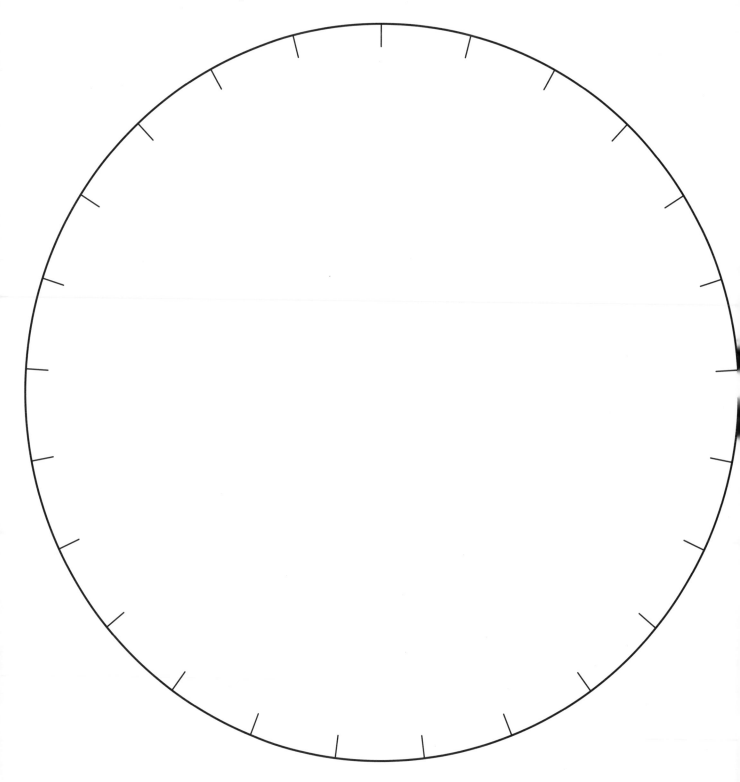

Cardboard Shuttle Template

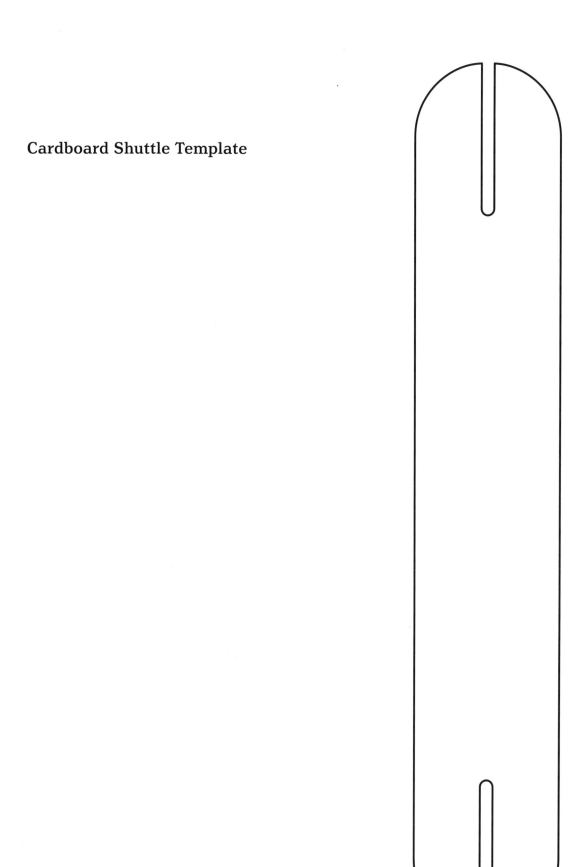

Index

To my grandmothers, who
inspired my love of fibre art.

First published in 2022 by
Search Press Limited
Wellwood, North Farm Road,
Tunbridge Wells, Kent TN2 3DR

ISBN: 978-1-80092-078-1
ebook ISBN: 978-1-80093-069-8

Extra copies of the templates are available from:
www.bookmarkedhub.com

This book was conceived, designed, and produced by
Quarto Publishing, an imprint of The Quarto Group
6 Blundell Street
London N7 9BH

Editor: Emma Harverson
Designer: Rachel Cross
Photographer: Nicki Dowey
Author portraits: Shannon Pierce Photography
Art Director: Gemma Wilson
Publisher: Lorraine Dickey

Printed and bound in China

10 9 8 7 6 5 4 3 2 1